THE BODY WHISPERER

YOUR SYMPTOMS TELL ME YOUR TRUTH

CHRISTINE LANG

The information in this book is not meant to be a substitute for professional medical care. Medical intuition does not diagnose illness nor does it prescribe specific medical treatment. It is not psychotherapy. If you have a serious medical or emotional problem, please see your physician or other licensed practitioner.

Typically human illnesses cannot be reduced to a single physical or emotional cause. Many nutritional, environmental, and other unknown reasons contribute to the development of illness and disease. Each person must work with their practitioners to determine which relationships, habits and stressors in their lives are contributing to health and to disease.

The intent of the author is to offer information to help you in your quest for emotional and spiritual well-being. The intuitive sessions presented in this book are frequently composites of several similar readings. Please assume that any similarity to a real person's name or situation is coincidental.

Contents

Preface

W e each see the world through a different lens. The colors on your lens are a composite of your upbringing, life experiences, and your character. When it comes to money, I may see the world through rose-colored glasses, while your lens may be a muddy brown in that topic area. How we live in the world depends on how opaque or transparent our lens is, allowing us to accurately perceive our life. I believe that a powerful journey—spiritual or otherwise—results in an improvement of one's lens; a clearing of the dark colors and the addition of positive, more transparent hues. My spiritual journey was unplanned, as so many are, and I was introduced to a new way of seeing the world while pursuing a cure for my allergies.

Sometimes I explain what I see in terms of television channels. If I ask you to describe the color of the wall in front of you and then ask you to describe its texture, you may feel like you "change channels" in your brain in order to register the different types of information. Most of us go through life with the equivalent of basic cable—we "see" what we can readily observe through our five senses. Nearly twenty years ago, I learned that there are hundreds of other channels available to us if we make the effort to tune in to them. Once you believe that these channels exist, you can begin developing the ability to tune in to them.

As a lawyer, I was trained to look for what was already wrong and what could go wrong. During my healing journey, I learned that the skills that made me a good lawyer—like the ability to spot a potential problem almost anywhere—made me a rather negative and unhappy person. I was difficult to please as I always saw room for improvement—in myself and in situations. My bosses may have enjoyed my perfectionist style, but my escalating allergies were my body's form of protest.

Learning to see the world energetically has meant understanding that the Universe is perfect just as it is. Given the mass suffering that happens daily on this planet, this approach may seem delusional, but over the last two decades, I've been privileged to sit with thousands of clients and speak to their spirits while They explain the grace behind each instance of suffering the client has endured. No injury happens without planning on the part of the Universe; there is intentionality behind each event. Every occurrence happens as part of a greater agenda, orchestrated by every spirit involved. Nothing occurs that does not in some way benefit everyone concerned. It's very common for clients to arrive not able to fathom how their pain could be of benefit to anyone. It's equally common for them to leave my treatment room in awe of the complex orchestration behind the events in their lives.

My statements are not meant to imply that suffering does not exist. Suffering is very real and invites us to have compassion for ourselves and for others. But we can think of instances where suffering is necessary and produces great miracles: the suffering of childbirth or the bittersweet suffering of watching one's child leave for his first day of kindergarten or college. We can recognize this suffering as painful but important, and I assert that your spirit views every instance of your suffering this way. Many years later most people can list the gifts that grew out of a painful situation, but at the time, they could only perceive the pain. It's my job to hold onto the larger perspective/truth while feeling compassion for the suffering occurring in the present moment.

My enhanced way of viewing the world has brought me a deep peace that comes from knowing that the world is not random and cruel. I still have stress—most definitely! But within a short period of time, I can reorient myself back into my knowing that every moment of stress serves as a compass helping me find my way back to my truth. I can resent the stress, or I can get quiet and still for a moment and feel the wisdom that is being offered to me. It is my hope that the stories offered here will convey some of what I've learned from the spirits that I've had the privilege of speaking with over the years and afford you some of this same sense of peace and knowing.

On a practical note: The stories in this book are not literally true in every detail. Names and identifying features of each client have been changed in order to protect their privacy. I've tried to write about issues that I see frequently among my clients and within my own life in the hopes that these are issues that will also apply to readers. There are friends and family members who've allowed me to use their actual names in this book. They are Joe, Thomas, Dana, Sandy, and my boys Joey and Justin. Please assume that every other name used throughout this book is fictional.

And lastly, I would like to pass along advice that the Buddha gave to his students (forgive my paraphrasing). He advised them to try on his teachings like a pair of shoes. If they did not seem like a good fit, then they should leave them behind. I believe that there is no one correct religion, spiritual practice, or belief system. My hope is that each person's beliefs guide them to be happy, empowered, and compassionate. If this is your result, then I don't care if you worship chocolate (and some people seem to).

Chapter 1

Becoming a Body Whisperer

"Madonna adopts George Clooney's love child!" was the headline I pretended not to read as I stood in line at the grocery store. As the person in front of me pushed her loaded cart towards the parking lot, I made eye contact with the cashier and smiled. Immediately I noticed a band of red energy across her forehead. It looked painful, and I squinted without realizing it. The cashier raised an eyebrow and asked, "Are you okay, Ma'am?"

I answered without thinking (a bad habit that I don't recommend), "I'm okay, but do you have a headache?"

"Yes!" she exclaimed, rubbing her forehead. I glanced down and noticed that she had dark, negative energy in her pelvic area, which I often see when people feel a lack of power in some way.

"Did something happen today that made you feel powerless?" I ventured.

"Yeah! I got a speeding ticket today that I totally didn't deserve! The guy in front of me was going way faster than I was and— Hey, wait!" she interrupted herself and looked confused for a second. "How did you know that I had a headache?"

Yes, how did I know that? And how was I going to explain what I was seeing? And why did I keep putting myself in these situations? I really needed to train myself not to jump in and offer help when it wasn't requested. To fully explain how I knew she had a headache would take a long time, and the customers in line behind me looked impatient, so I opted for a short answer.

"I can see energy, and I don't have time now to tell you much more, but if I can put some energy into your abdomen, your headache will probably diminish."

She looked hesitant. "I can't really leave this register...and there's a line of customers."

The lady in line behind me scowled, warning us to not even mention the possibility of delaying her.

"Ughhh, gross," said the teenaged bag boy packing my groceries. He had been absorbed in what I was saying and not paying attention, and he'd smashed my eggs with a carton of milk. He looked up sheepishly and said, "I'm sorry, Ma'am. I'll go to the back of the store and get you more eggs."

I recognized an opportunity when I saw it, and I quickly moved around behind the counter while the guy ran off to get the eggs. I used my hands to place some healing energy into the cashier and felt her sigh with relief as her body began to unclench in response to the positive energy flowing into her body. Just as I finished, the bag boy returned with my eggs, the cashier finished ringing me up, and I left.

For the next two months whenever that cashier saw me heading to the checkout area, she would wave her hand and say, "Over here! Over here! This register's open!" I learned to avoid her because she would flood me with questions like: "Who do you think will win homecoming queen at my school?" "Do you know the winning lottery numbers?" "Do you think that I'll do well on my history final?" "What color is my energy when I think of Bobby?" Situations like these are how I've trained myself (slowly, I admit) to think before I open my mouth about what I perceive in people.

I wasn't always this way. I was raised by entrepreneurial parents, and I thought of myself as someone who came from a smart and successful gene pool. I grew up valuing intelligence, power, and money—probably in that order. I went to college and law school, and after graduating law school, I fell in love with a man who lived in Charlotte, North Carolina. We got married, and I moved to the South and practiced law as an in-house lawyer for a large bank. I was on my way to a great life, according to all the American standards I grew up with.

But during my first year of law school, I developed allergies. My doctor said I was allergic to dust, which exists everywhere (I think even on the moon!). So my choices were: 1) to take antihistamines each day, which made me very drowsy, or 2) to carry around a box of tissues and blow my nose constantly. (This was before the days of the drugs we have now which don't cause drowsiness.) I alternated between these two options for a couple of years, using caffeine to combat the drowsiness and whining about how much mucous the body could produce when not held back by antihistamines.

I was thrilled when my doctor recommended a steroid-based inhaler that suppressed my allergies to the point that they seemed to disappear. Everything was great until I talked to my doctor about getting pregnant and was told that I would have to give up my steroid inhaler once I got pregnant. That's when the stubborn, demanding lawyer side of me took over, and I refused to go back to blowing my nose 150 times a day.

I had been to rural China on business trips with my husband and watched hundreds of women working in rice fields. None of them were carrying tissue boxes, and I was pretty sure that there was no local store carrying steroid-based inhalers. So what were *they* using for allergy relief? I began studying Chinese herbs and was encouraged by the concept of retraining my immune system instead of just trying to suppress my body's allergic reactions.

In the early 1980s a reliable source of Chinese herbs was not easy to find in my town, so I began to investigate homeopathic medicine. I studied homeopathy like I was pursuing another law degree, attending conferences and study groups and reading dozens of books. Using homeopathic remedies and what I learned about rebalancing the body, I was able to get rid of approximately fifty percent of my allergies. I still needed some tissues, but I knew that I was on the right track. I began recommending homeopathic remedies to friends and family members, and their various symptoms improved as well.

The relief that homeopathy provided convinced me that energy medicine was real, and so I plunged into the study of energy. I read books on quantum physics, feeling more comfortable with "hard science" than anything metaphysical. I came from a background that valued analytical reasoning, and most metaphysical books seemed too "airy-fairy" for me. But when I began taking tai chi lessons from a woman who seemed incredibly peaceful, I had to look at spirituality differently. Don't get me wrong, I was still the cynical lawyer, but there was no denying that when I spent time around this teacher, I felt different. More relaxed, calm, and somehow... safer. I began hanging around after class, and my instructor taught me about Taoism and living in balance. I began meditating, which was comical at first because my brain, so long worshipped by me, refused to quiet down. I wanted more answers, so I began studying Buddhism in addition to Taoism. The books, retreats, and workshops began making a real difference in how I felt, so I continued to meditate daily, even though on some days my busy mind offered me more frustration than inner peace.

My career took a strange turn at this point. I left the practice of law to become a business consultant. One of my first clients was a veterinarian, and in chatting with him, I mentioned that I'd trained dogs and horses while I was in college. Before I realized what I was saying, I'd agreed to teach a dog-obedience class at his vet clinic. I thought it was a one-time thing, so I had fun with it, making people laugh and enjoying training the dogs and their owners. To my surprise, the class was a huge hit, and the receptionist at the vet's office told me that there was a waiting list to take my next class. "Next class?" I asked incredulously.

I went home and thought about it and realized that I was hesitating about teaching more classes because it would likely mean choosing to be a dog trainer instead of a lawyer and business consultant. This seemed like a lot to give up. Graduating from a prestigious California law school had given me instant credentials, a sort of name tag that said, "Pay attention—I'm a lawyer, which means that I'm smart and powerful." Telling people I was a dog trainer conveyed little of the same impressive ideas—hell, it didn't even convey that I went to college.

My husband encouraged me to follow my heart, and I had to admit that dog training was so fun and easy, I was surprised that people were paying me so much to do it. So what began as a favor for a client blossomed into a local phenomenon, with me teaching classes five nights a week and getting referrals from most of the local vets, dog groomers, and animal-control officers. I made more money as a dog trainer than I did as a lawyer, which also helped to validate my decision. And teaching dog-obedience classes at night meant that I was free during the day to pursue my other passions—studying alternative medicines and Eastern religions.

At my tai chi instructor's suggestion, I took a Reiki class. The purpose of the class was to teach me to channel healing energy through my hands and into my own body or someone else's body to facilitate healing. I have to admit that ten minutes into the workshop, my inner lawyer reared her ugly head and scoffed at the "hocus-pocus" style of teaching that the Reiki teacher employed. I came home doubtful that any real transformation had occurred and didn't try to work with healing energy for over a year.

About fourteen months later I was in San Francisco and watched a man performing energy healing on someone. A light bulb went off, and I "knew" or recognized that I had the same ability, and that it was time to start using it. With my interest and faith in energy healing reignited, I went home and began offering energy treatments to friends. While the energy treatments seemed to help alleviate their symptoms for awhile, invariably the symptoms would come back, and the friends would be back at my door asking for another treatment.

In an effort to be more focused while offering an energy treatment, I started meditating beforehand. I found that after meditating, I felt more certain about where to place the energy, and the healing seemed to last a bit longer. Then I began noticing that as I sat in meditation, a phrase or an image would float into my mind. I would usher it away like the other thoughts, but this one would keep floating back into my awareness. It was gentle, not agitated like my usual thoughts, and seemed nurturing somehow. I wondered if these pictures and phrases applied to the friend that I was about to channel energy into, and I began relaying the "messages" to my friends, asking if they made sense to them. To my surprise, the given phrase would usually elicit an "ah-ha" moment, and my friends would experience a revelation that seemed to correspond to the injury or ailment causing them suffering. And then the healing would hold—sometimes permanently!

This was the answer I was looking for about why energy healing—and so many forms of healing— only lasted a short time. There seemed to be an emotional connection that needed to be addressed in order for the body to "release" the symptom. And somehow I was being given this important information...by someone.

I sat in meditation in the hopes that this mysterious "helpful stranger" would reveal Herself to me. I raised my energy up to the middle of my forehead (the third-eye location) as I had been taught by my meditation teachers. Then I felt my energy being gently nudged up higher until it sat just above my head. And then I heard a soft voice say, "Welcome home." I began to cry without understanding why. My spirit introduced Herself. She told me that we all receive guidance from our spirit, or soul, all the time. This guidance usually comes as "feelings" and occurs in our heart area, which is one of two "portals" through which we receive information from our spirit. The other portal is located above the head (also known as the 7th chakra), which is why She helped me move my energy up to that opening. She informed me that I could ask Her any question, and She would try to give me an answer that I could understand.

For the next six months, I was like a kid in a candy store! I sat in meditation for three to four hours a day, pummeling my ever-patient spirit with questions about everything. "Why is there suffering in the world?" "Why do we age instead of just dropping over dead when we hit 100?" "Why do some people seem to have easier lives?" "Did God make a mistake when designing body parts that sag?" (No, all of my questions were not profound.) And in between my barrage of questions, my spirit got Her "lessons" in, teaching me about the Universe and about illness, emotions, and healing. When I doubted myself and wondered if I was really hearing Her or just going crazy, She would direct me to a bookstore and a specific book and a specific page. And there on the specified page would be the very information that I had channeled earlier that day! My doubts would recede for awhile, and I would be back on my meditation cushion.

The friends who had experienced seemingly miraculous recoveries after receiving both energy and a message from me told some of their friends. And they told a few more friends, and soon complete strangers were calling me and asking for help. I was delighted to help, as these treatments gave my spirit a way to continue teaching me about emotional patterns present within different symptoms and how to promote healing.

Because I was still employed as a dog trainer, I sometimes worked with dogs and their owners privately in their homes. As I spent more time during the day meditating, I became more skillful at holding that calm, peaceful space when I left my meditation room. As a result, I was more perceptive and intuitive about the dogs and about their owners. I could perceive the source of an underlying anxiety in a dog, and frequently I could look at the dog owner and "know" something about her life or her physical body. Being the big mouth that I am, I usually blurted out what I perceived about the person. Soon many of my dog-training appointments were spent completely ignoring the poor dog as I talked to the owner about the emotional stressors that were contributing to her physical symptoms. Once when the phone rang and the caller asked for an appointment, I had to ask, "Are you wanting help for your dog or help with healing yourself?" The awkward pause on the other end of the phone was embarrassing but helped me realize that it was time to close the dog-training business and concentrate on my healing work.

So I laugh when folks ask me if they should follow the path I took to become an intuitive because I'm hesitant to say, "Well, first you go to law school, then you become a dog trainer, and then you start hearing your spirit and She trains you, and..."

I guess my journey proves that you can get here from anywhere.

Chapter 2

Carolyn's Case – Life on a Hamster's Wheel

Carolyn arrived ten minutes late for her first session with me. She appeared flustered and apologized repeatedly for being late, talking rapidly while rushing towards the treatment room as if she could make up for lost time. She was well dressed and looked professional and stylish. She talked while she filled out the information form I hand to new clients, and I marveled at her ability to simultaneously write and speak at such a fast speed. She told me that she worked for a large corporation in the city and that her career was going very well. The reason she had sought me out for a session was to shed some light on her physical symptoms, which were fatigue, eczema, and digestion issues.

I asked Carolyn what she understood about her symptoms. She said that she'd been checked out by her doctor and told that there did not appear to be any major problems with her health. He had given her acid inhibitors for her digestion problems and a steroid-based cream for her eczema. Her fatigue he attributed to "stress," and he advised her to try and get more sleep.

I then asked her for a few sentences about her childhood, including a description of her parents. Carolyn thought for a moment, and then said, "I'm the oldest of four children, and I guess my mom counted on me to help run the household. Dad was a pharmacist—a quiet, strong man—and when he got home, he liked to have time alone to read the paper." Carolyn also said that she remembered her mother always being happy. Carolyn had earned good grades at school and had gone to a prestigious college, where she'd excelled.

When asked about her current personal life, Carolyn said that she'd been married to Bill for twenty-one years, and that their two children (aged 13 & 17) were wonderful. Bill used to work in the banking industry and was a successful, happy man when Carolyn married him. He had lost his job during a merger and over the years had experienced a run of bad luck finding a career that suited him. He was now working part-time in a clerical position and was pursuing photography, which he enjoyed but had never made money doing. Carolyn confessed that she would love to cut back on her sixty-hour work week, but that the family needed the high salary she earned.

"I guess we're a pretty typical family, worrying about money and wishing we had more of it. But that's everyone's story, right?" she asked. "People always wish that they could work fewer hours and make more money."

When I raised my energy up high enough, I could

hear Carolyn's spirit, and She talked to me about Carolyn's childhood. I learned that Carolyn watched her mom work tirelessly to take care of the family and meet everyone's needs, rarely expressing any needs of her own. So the model that Carolyn had of what an ideal woman should be was "a hard worker who happily gets it all done." But "getting it all done" now included earning most of the money, as well as running the household and taking care of the children.

Carolyn's spirit said more. *"Carolyn's perception of her mother as always happy means that she holds this standard for herself, and so she doesn't want to feel that she burdens anyone with her own needs. To admit to feelings of unhappiness would be seen by Carolyn as evidence that she is failing at running her life well. So instead of asking for help when her list of duties becomes too extensive, Carolyn simply pushes herself harder. The fatigue is physical and emotional. Physically she is not always getting enough rest due to very long work days, and emotionally Carolyn feels very fatigued because she doesn't see an end in sight."*

I opened my eyes (I typically close them when I'm listening to someone's spirit so that I can fully focus on what I'm hearing) and saw tears running down Carolyn's face.

"She's right you know—my spirit. I do feel like there's no end in sight. I mean, what's going to change? Bill's become so discouraged about potential job openings that he seems apathetic and disengaged from the world. He has a part-time job that brings in a tiny bit of money, but I think he's given up on ever being a significant bread winner again."

Carolyn's spirit chimed in, *"And more importantly, he has given up on feeling empowered. He's content to let Carolyn be the only one who feels empowered in their partnership."*

As I relayed this statement to Carolyn, I watched her shoulders droop as she gave in to her feelings of emotional exhaustion. "Bill's a good man, he really is," she said quickly. "It's just that he's had some bad luck with work, and now he seems to have just quit trying. He's content to work in this job that is so beneath his abilities. And he's good at photography, but when people have suggested ways for him to make money with it, he's ignored their suggestions. He has said in the past that he's wanted to take pictures for a living, so his actions—or lack of them—don't make sense to me!"

Carolyn's spirit gently offered, *"If your husband enjoys photography, but he resists doing it in a way that earns money then it sounds like a hobby. Hobbies are fine to pursue as long as you're also meeting your other obligations. Is it alright for him to spend large portions of each day on his hobby while you're working full time and also doing most of the work with the children and the household?"*

At this question, Carolyn burst into tears. "It isn't fair, is it?" she cried. "I know that he's been somewhat depressed, and I like that he seems happier when he's taking pictures, but why is he not wondering what will make me happy, and the kids? They're aware of the financial pressure that keeps me working full-time, and they see their dad as weak for letting me work so hard to provide all of our money."

"*And that,*" Carolyn's spirit said, "*is why you have digestive issues. This situation is literally hard for you to digest. You don't like how you and your children are seeing your husband, and it's eating at you because you don't know how to talk to Bill about it.*"

"Yes! I brought it up once, and he just got defensive, went out to the garage, and didn't talk much for the next few days. Talking to him doesn't work, so I feel like I have no choice but to just live with it until he decides to change."

Carolyn's spirit told her that all of her symptoms were an expression of her dissatisfaction with her current situation. Her eczema was a way of her body telling her that "something was getting under her skin," namely the fact that she couldn't talk to her husband about what was bothering her. When we're forced to shut down and hold our feelings inside, then we cease to have a true partnership, and Carolyn's irritation at this fact was understandable. When her spirit spoke of losing a sense of partnership, Carolyn began to cry again.

"It's true. I used to be able to talk to Bill about anything, and he was a great problem solver. Now he seems so fragile and negative, so I don't feel that I can ask him for help in solving problems, especially when he's part of the problem and doesn't want to hear about that. And I don't want to talk to my family about it because I don't want them to think less of Bill. So I just hold it in—and scratch this eczema!"

Carolyn's spirit told her that her stomach

issues stemmed from the negative feelings she had about herself. The stomach area is frequently where we register negative thoughts about how we view ourselves and how we believe that others see us. Because her memories of her mother were of a woman who was always happy, Carolyn felt like a failure when she felt too drained to engage with her children and husband. She had learned from childhood that a "good mother and wife" was always cheerful, energetic, and happy to support her family and meet their needs. While intellectually Carolyn could admit that no one is always happy, emotionally she felt disappointed in herself whenever she expressed negative emotions to her family.

Carolyn also felt guilt about her lack of sexual interest in her husband. Her spirit explained that the sexual attraction in her marriage was partially based on respect and admiration, and that Carolyn had lost respect for her husband. Once again the tears flowed as Carolyn admitted for the first time out loud that she had lost respect for Bill.

"I feel so guilty saying this, but part of me wants to yell at him to 'man up' and help support his family. He's really not taking care of us in any way—financially or emotionally. And as soon as I have that thought, I feel terrible for thinking that way because I'm being critical instead of being a supportive wife."

"*Perhaps,*" Carolyn's spirit said, "*you need to look at your beliefs about what support really means. Support doesn't always mean saying and doing whatever makes that person happy and comfortable. It should also mean speaking your truth and helping*

*the people you love to be the best that they can be.
If you defined support that way, how would that
change things for you?"*

Carolyn thought for a moment, then slowly
ventured, "I...would tell him that he could be more
than what he is right now, and that I haven't avoided
sex with him because I've stopped loving him, but
maybe because he's stopped loving himself, and he
acts so pessimistic."

"Very good!" Carolyn's spirit said. *"Now you're
using your truth to truly support yourself and your
husband. What else would you tell him?"*

Emboldened by the opportunity to speak her
truth and be validated, Carolyn smiled and added,
"I would tell him that I need for him to earn at least
half of what I earn by the end of this year so that I
can cut my hours back a bit." Quickly the big smile
was replaced by a look of apprehension. "But what
if he gets angry and defensive or shuts down and
doesn't talk to me for days?"

Carolyn's spirit asked, *"If you had to talk to
your daughter about her grades being less than you
thought she was capable of, would you skip having
the conversation because you were worried about
her potential reaction?"*

"No," Carolyn said quickly, "that's my job as a
parent, to help my children do their best. Oh, I see!
That's also my job as a partner and best friend to
my husband, to call him on his behavior when it's
causing him to not do his best."

*"Yes, and it's part of your job as a parent to
help the other parent see when he's not modeling
the healthiest behavior to his children. Right now*

your husband's defeated attitude is teaching your children that sometimes life beats you down, and you can't ever recover. And that sometimes one person has to take care of another person for as long as he sees himself as weak and unable to compete in the world. Are these beliefs that you want your children to have?"

"No! I want my son to be strong and capable—like my dad is, and like my husband used to be," said Carolyn.

This is when Carolyn's spirit pointed out to her that her energy level had shot way up.

"You're right!" she exclaimed. "I feel so much better! But why is that? Nothing has changed."

This answer I knew without even channeling Carolyn's spirit. "Because so much of your exhaustion was the belief that you had no good options available to you, and that you couldn't even speak to anyone about how stuck you felt. You saw your options as: 1) be the supportive wife, accept the current situation, and remain miserable, or 2) be the complaining, unsupportive wife, and feel guilty. But when you spoke your truth and heard feedback from your spirit, you began to see that other options exist. *Whenever we feel stuck, it's because we don't see an option that feels empowering.* Your spirit is always ready to offer more options that you aren't seeing."

I gave Carolyn an energy treatment even though she insisted that she was already feeling better, and she made an appointment for another session in two weeks.

Chapter 3

Susan's Case – The Body's Wisdom

My next session was with a woman named Susan. Susan had breast cancer four years ago and had been experiencing a variety of symptoms ever since. None of her symptoms were as life-threatening as cancer, but they were causing her to see her doctors frequently.

I'm always pleased to work with clients who have already consulted their doctor regarding their symptoms. The Universe's rule seems to be that once a client has pursued the diagnostic tools used in Western medicine and is still suffering, then I'm able to access information on the situation. I think this "rule" exists because when I first discovered my abilities, clients would come to me instead of seeing their doctor and ask me to serve as their diagnostician. This was usually because the client was afraid of doctors, and my spirit did not want to help perpetuate such fear-based avoidance.

Since my primary job is to help people understand the emotional factors present within their symptoms, my spirit said that I was not to focus too heavily on diagnosing. This has been accomplished by the Universe showing me a blank screen if the client asks me about a symptom that she has not yet spoken to her doctor about. This doesn't apply to minor symptoms, but certainly applies when a client asks me to check her out and see if she has cancer or some other serious illness. Since Susan regularly saw doctors and other practitioners, I felt confident that her spirit would be happy to shed light on her various symptoms.

Susan had seen her gynecologist for chronic yeast infections and bladder infections, her chiropractor for frequent adjustments, and her family doctor for chronic colds that had progressed to sinus infections. She was also spending a lot of money at health-food stores, buying supplements that she had read about on the internet or heard about from friends. Susan arrived for her first session with a large duffle bag filled with her regimen of daily supplements.

I let Susan give me a brief description of her medical history, and I could feel the fear in her as she spoke. Instead of asking more questions, I decided to connect to Susan's spirit and let Her direct the session.

Susan's spirit began by asking her a question. *"What was your mother's belief about illness and how the body heals itself?"*

Susan looked confused, which was understandable. I was experienced in these types of conversations, and even I wasn't completely sure where this was going.

"Well, I guess she believed in going to the doctor

if you got sick and taking the medicines the doctors gave her. Is that what you mean?"

Her spirit tried another approach, telling me to ask her which statement sounded more like something that her mother would say:

1. The body usually heals itself if given time and the right support, or

2. Once the body is compromised—by age or by illness—it's never the same again.

Susan's eyes lit up. "Oh! The second sentence—definitely. That sounds exactly like something that my mom would say. Why?"

"Because," her spirit said, *"you have learned from your mother how to view your body, and you're now under the impression that your body is damaged or weakened in some way, and that it will never be strong again."*

Susan pondered that idea for a moment. "No, I don't think that's right. I think that I'm pretty healthy. I do lots of reading—online and in books—about the latest research on supplements and nutrition. And I eat well and exercise."

Her spirit replied, *"And if Christine asks you to leave that large bag of supplements here for the next week, how healthy will you be?"*

"Well, no. I can't do that. These vitamins and herbs are important."

"When you were a teenager, did you take vitamins and other supplements?"

"No," Susan said cautiously.

"And yet your body still figured out how to

remain healthy and even how to grow into an adult woman—all without the help of supplements. How did it do that?"

"Oh," Susan said quietly. "I guess my body just knew what to do. Maybe because I was healthier back then or stronger."

"And do you think that this wisdom, this knowledge of how to function, how to heal, has been taken from your body?" her spirit asked.

"I don't know!" Susan replied defensively. "I just keep watching things go wrong with my body, and each problem needs a different supplement or prescription medicine to fix it."

Patiently her spirit continued. *"The problem is not that your body forgot how to fix itself. The problem is that you lost confidence in your body's ability to heal itself. During your childhood, your mother taught you, through small comments and actions, that it's possible that your body will 'break down' in some way, and that once that happens, you'll never again have that intelligent body you had in childhood that repaired itself without your help.*

"When you were diagnosed with cancer, you entered that 'other' category, the one that your mom lived in, where the body is permanently deficient and needs help to function. Your belief, at the subconscious level, is that once you're in that category, you're in it for life. So now you're expecting your body to function with difficulties, and your brain is directing it to do just that."

"How am I directing my body to be sick?" Susan asked desperately.

Her spirit, sounding gentle and kind as all spirits

do, asked another question. *"Have you heard that approximately every six years you replace every cell in your body?"*

"Yes, I have heard that. I think I've read that in a couple of different books," Susan answered.

"Well, if every cell in your body gets replaced over a six-year period, then how does a man who injures his knee playing high-school football still have knee pain twenty years later?"

"Uh...I don't know. I never thought of it that way before. Hmm...that doesn't make sense, does it? So why does that happen?"

"It happens because the man's brain directs the cells to reproduce exactly as they are—injured or weakened. This is because the man doesn't expect his knee to be fully functional like it was before the injury. And the brain, in directing each cell to duplicate itself, is guided by the beliefs that are held in the mind.

"There are times when an injury does not fully heal because a surgery was done poorly or there is a complicating issue that blocks complete healing. But when such factors are not present, a person may still fail to experience complete healing because his expectations direct the body's healing process, and too often people fear that a complete recovery is impossible.

"The population provides examples of complete healing, and it provides even more examples of your mother's belief, which is that damaged body parts usually don't heal completely, especially in older people. Your ego will find evidence of whatever it is looking for. Unfortunately our egos usually look

for evidence that our 'worst-case-scenario' is true. And when we find that evidence, we use it to bolster our fear-based belief, and then our brain directs our body to follow that limiting idea.

"Your body is capable of complete healing from the cancer and from your other symptoms, and it's equally capable of not fully healing. In taking all of these supplements, you are sending the message to your body that you now believe it to be weak—too weak to function unaided."

A look of panic washed across Susan's face. "Are you telling me that in order to get well, I have to give up all my supplements because otherwise I'm telling my body that it's weak, and I will keep getting sick?"

"Nothing drastic needs to be done today," her spirit said soothingly. *"The goal is to help you gain enough confidence in your body and its wisdom that you begin feeling safe in not taking some of the supplements. As your confidence in your body increases, the number of supplements you feel are necessary will decrease. But as long as you believe that your body is weak and needing assistance from supplements, then you are advised to take them. Together we will work on rebuilding your confidence in what your body can accomplish. This is a process, and there's no rush."*

Susan's relief was palpable. I reassured her that no one was asking her to completely transform her beliefs in one day. We can change our mental understandings quickly, but it usually takes time for us to really feel a new truth on the emotional level. And when we feel something as our emotional reality, we act on it naturally, not because we feel forced. As long as you're feeling that you "should" do something, it's not your emotional truth yet; it's still a mental belief. I told Susan that she didn't need to stop taking her supplements until she felt intuitively that she didn't need each particular product.

Susan pondered that notion, then asked another question. "So is the goal here to have me stop taking all supplements because then it will mean that I have complete faith in my body?"

"That's a good question," her spirit responded encouragingly, *"and the answer is no. The goal is not to refrain from taking all supplements. Living in your world subjects the body to environmental stressors, and your food, even if you eat a very healthy diet, is usually lacking in some nutrients. For these reasons you may derive benefit from supplementing your diet. But the goal is to lessen your fears and establish enough trust in your body so that you can use your intuition to feel which supplements would benefit you at any given time.*

"As the body ages, its needs change, and the ideal situation is one where the individual can be informed about vitamins and nutrients that may be missing from her diet and to be able to feel if it is time to add these supplements to her diet."

Susan's spirit also reminded her that she grew from a little bundle of cells into a baby, which grew into a toddler, a teen, and then an adult. The wisdom within her cells that guided that process did not evaporate or expire, it remains within her. As she recognizes the wisdom within her, she invites it to come forward again to guide her health, rather than letting her fears play such a large role in directing her body's daily operations.

Susan left her session feeling optimistic but looking a little unsettled. This can happen when we challenge long-held beliefs; it can shake our foundation and leave us feeling a bit ungrounded. It takes courage to be patient with this feeling of shifting to a new truth, and many people revert back to their old patterns of thinking in order to feel stable again. But Susan was motivated to work through her feelings of uneasiness at being outside of her comfort zone since she understood that her beliefs were contributing to her symptoms. We agreed to meet again in two weeks, and I recommended some books for her to read to present herself with evidence that her long-standing beliefs might not be accurate.

Chapter 4

Being a Single Woman & an Intuitive

I n case you're developing an image of me as this wise, ever-peaceful woman, I should share a bit about my life these days. I've been divorced from my ex-husband for nine years, and we live fairly close to each other. Our two boys, aged 16 and 18, spend three and a half days with each of us, and we manage this process quite well. Actually, I would venture to say that we still parent very well together. Our primary focus has always been the kids, and in general we support each other and communicate well.

That's the good stuff. The bad stuff is that ten years ago we moved as a family from North Carolina, where I had plenty of friends and a thriving practice, to southern California. We moved out here to be near my family and to grow my business. We had the very mistaken idea that because people were seen as more progressive in California, I would enjoy even more success with my abilities in California than in North Carolina. Unfortunately my business grew very slowly here because there are so many hypnotists, tarot-card readers, psychics, energy healers, etc. that the market is saturated with alternative practitioners. I imagine that it's difficult for the average person to wade through the myriad of "healers" and find someone who is truly talented and appropriate for the type of healing that's needed.

Within a year of moving to California, my husband and I realized that we had grown apart, and we separated. I was no longer the power-seeking, aggressive attorney that he married, and he was a very different person too. We had grown in seemingly opposite directions, and neither of us had a desire to turn back or move towards the other person's perspective of the world. He could appreciate my passion for spiritual development, teaching, and healing work, but he didn't want it to be such a prominent part of his life. I wanted to move away from the fear-based way that I saw most people living, where they worked hard to stay disconnected from their true feelings, keeping themselves distracted with food, shopping, and other stimulations. My ex said that he liked feeling like everyone else and didn't want to feel different than the "typical American experience," and so we found ourselves seeking different paths.

While I live more successfully with an ex-husband than most women I know, life as a divorced woman with my abilities can be rather...interesting. When it comes to dating men, I find that either my intuition is too "on," and I'm knowing more about a man than I want to know on the first date, or my intuition is completely "off," and I say yes to a second date with someone who is totally wrong for me. I'm upfront with men that I meet, telling them honestly about my abilities and how I earn a living. I've had men run away from me like their pants were on fire and others who were intrigued and asked genuine questions. I've had men decide that my abilities could be useful to them and then ask for my help picking cars, finding investors, and dealing with troublesome family members. I even had a man, apparently mistaking me for Samantha on *Bewitched*, ask if I would put a "spell" on his ex-wife (my answer was no).

Everyone has intuition. Imagine walking into your kitchen and seeing your two friends doing the dishes. They're not speaking and their body language is typical for people washing dishes, but you know that they were arguing before you walked in. How do you know this? I would suggest that it's because you can feel the negative energy around them and between them. Body language will certainly give you information, but the fastest perception ability that you have is your ability to instantly feel another person's energy.

Intuition is simply the experience of knowing something without the use of logic or reasoning. We all have it—I just seem to have a lot of it, and I've focused on developing mine more than most people have. I use the analogy of Michael Jordan playing basketball. We can all play basketball to some degree; he just plays at a different level than the rest of us. But if you played with him for awhile, he could definitely improve your game. Everyone can become more intuitive with some guidance and practice.

And my intuition isn't always guaranteed to be "on." If I get really focused on accomplishing a mundane task, like getting the kids to school on time, then I can be as dense as a brick and seem to have no intuition. I have to remind myself to slow down and pay attention to my feelings and intuition, just like I tell my students to do.

My kids have some of my abilities too. Not because I've crafted miniature versions of myself, but because we all have these abilities as babies, and I've helped my boys retain their sensitivities. I believe that we can all see energy when we're infants. My spirit says that babies can see the colors in our energy field, and that this is how they get information about people before they understand language. I've watched a baby fuss when handed to one person then smile when passed to a different person. When I looked at the first person's energy field, sure enough she had a lot of dark energy around her, relaying that she was feeling strong negative emotions.

As toddlers, we learn that everything that is real has a name. When no one describes the colors we see around people, we chalk that up to something our imagination is creating, and we pull our attention away from it. As we all know from our experiences with trying to remember algebra, if you don't use certain brain connections regularly, they fade. When I teach energy perception classes to teenagers and adults, I'm amazed at how much faster kids learn to see energy. Maybe it's because it's been longer since the adults tried to use those neural pathways, and so it takes them longer to reawaken those skills. So from the time my kids were toddlers, I talked about the energy that I saw when we were out in public, and they've maintained their ability to see energy and be fairly intuitive.

My boys also seemed to learn much faster than I have about how and when to present "what you know." When they were younger and saw negative energy around a teacher, they waited until they got home to ask me about it. I'm surprised that they never asked the teacher directly about what they were seeing, but I guess that's more evidence of how their intuition was sharp from the beginning. I would have been tempted to approach the teacher and say, "Are you aware that your energy is really scattered and dark? What's troubling you?" But they always knew to hold onto their comments and questions until they got home. While we run errands, Justin might tell me that his teacher "felt and looked sad today," and I would know that he was referring to her energy as well as her facial expressions. And my oldest son, Joey, would always come home from his first day of the school year and describe his teachers by listing who had the most glowing energy, the calmest energy, etc. He had a way of getting great information about each teacher that I admired, so I encouraged him to pay attention to what he perceived. To my knowledge, the boys have never presented information that they picked up intuitively to someone who didn't ask for the information.

The same cannot be said about me. I have stumbled and bumbled my way through so many awkward conversations that began with me blurting out insights that, while they may have been accurate—even profound—they were completely unsolicited and usually unappreciated. I have had to learn through numerous mistakes that people don't always want the truth set before them, especially when that truth may require them to take action. Just as I've had to learn numerous skills from my spirit in order to perform the job that I have now, I've also had to learn to "read my audience." I now understand that part of my job is to build a bridge between what I understand and what my client knows. Sometimes we're not that far apart, but sometimes where my client sits and where I sit are miles apart, and I must move carefully as I present information to help my client see her life from her spirit's perspective, which is much larger than her current perspective.

I've also had to learn to separate out what I "want" to hear from what my spirit is actually telling me. The more I care about someone, the more invested I am in getting a particular answer, and the less "clear" I am. So it's harder for me to hear my child's spirit when he is sick than it is for me to hear the spirit of someone in the hospital that I don't know. I do want to help the person in the hospital, but his suffering doesn't affect me emotionally in the same way as my child's suffering, and so I'm able to be more "objective" and listen to his spirit without an internal agenda filtering what I'm hearing.

I guess this is also why my "hearing" (of my

spirit) can be so off when I'm asking my spirit for Her input on a man I'm interested in. If I think he looks like a real catch, then I tend to interpret every word and visual that She gives me through rose-colored glasses. So, for example, when I met a cute guy with a great career and a great sense of humor, I completely missed my spirit's warnings about his internal conflict. "Yeah, yeah, he's feeling conflict—I can help with that!" I thought each time I meditated and my spirit led me to that topic. But shortly after we began dating, I began to see that the cute guy dealt with his internal conflicts by drinking too much alcohol, and I had to look more carefully at what my spirit had been pointing to.

For years when I would experience something unpleasant, like meeting a man I was attracted to and then discovering he drank too much for my comfort, I would get angry with my spirit. "Why didn't You warn me?!" I would yell at Her internally. Sometimes I would also "quit" (this is embarrassing to admit), which means that I would refuse to sit in meditation and connect to my spirit. I would decide that She must enjoy tricking me or letting me fall on my face, or that the spirit world in general was not very helpful, and I would pull away. Sometimes my spirit would patiently wait until I got over my temper tantrum and reconnected with Her. Other times the Universe would tap me on the shoulder, which usually took the form of one of my kids getting sick or a friend having a physical symptom—some event that would draw me back towards my spirit's guidance. Then I would wrestle with the situation, knowing that meditation would bring me more answers than

I could get by using logic alone, but still reluctant to connect back to "my untrustworthy spirit."

I would always end up back on my meditation cushion, and my spirit would help me see the reasons why I wasn't simply fed all the answers so that I walked through life looking omniscient. (Although I still think that experiencing omniscience would be a blast!) I understand that I learn important things through my life experiences, and that if She just gave me all the answers, I would have mental comprehension but not experiential knowledge. The wisdom that we gain from our experiences becomes part of us and helps us deepen our compassion for others. I used to wish that my spirit would shield me from all negative events, but now I recognize the value of the deeper insights that I've gained through my experiences.

I no longer pull away from my spirit when things get painful. I don't accuse Her of not caring or tricking me, etc. Now I seek Her out as if She was an instruction manual for my life. I know that my spirit will offer guidance, comfort, and clarity that can help me move through my life with grace. My job is to stop taking things personally and getting upset because then I can't raise my energy in meditation and get centered enough to hear Her guidance. She's there ready to help, but I have to make the connection with Her.

Chapter 5

Dr. Stevenson – Medical Cases and a Yogi Infatuation

It's Thursday morning which means that Dr. Ann Stevenson will be here at 10 a.m. sharp. Dr. Stevenson has a standing appointment every Thursday. The first part of each session is spent asking her spirit questions about some of her patients, and the remaining time is devoted to personal guidance for Ann. At 10:01 the doorbell rings, and my standard poodle, Lola, cocks one eyebrow towards me to say, "Are you going to get that?"

This dog is even more intuitive than I am, and she always seems to know who's on the other side of the door. She almost never barks. If I don't hear the doorbell, she comes and finds me and stares at me, asking me why I'm not opening the door. The only people who cause her to bark are men that I'm not expecting. But as soon as I glance through the peephole of my door and know who it is, my energy must relax because she immediately stops barking.

A quick aside about how Lola came in to my life: Other than during my college years, I've always lived with a dog. During the divorce, I realized that my boys were missing their dog for the part of each week that they were spending at their dad's house. I decided that the kids should get custody of their dog since they'd already experienced enough loss, and so Kipper the dog began to follow the same custody schedule as my kids. So half of each week I was completely alone in the house.

Suddenly I had another level of loss in my life. I was just getting used to living without my children for a portion of each week, and now there were three days a week where my house was completely empty. I was startled by how strange it felt not to have furry feet padding around behind me. I decided to get another dog so that I had full-time canine companionship, and I began considering different breeds.

As a former dog trainer, I'm picky. I'm a sucker for a cute face, and funny-looking dogs like dachshunds make me laugh every time I see them, but if a dog's going to live with me, he has to be smart. Our other dog, Kipper, is smart, but unfortunately he uses his intelligence against me, not for me. When it comes to issues like food—people food or dog food—we are not on the same team. If a piece of food falls to the floor, it's every beast for himself, and Kipper moves faster than a cheetah on crack. He's figured out how to get up on dining-room chairs and eat off the table in the time it takes me to go to the bathroom, and then lies back down on the floor and looks innocent, as if that food just disappeared by itself. So for my next dog, I wanted a dog that would actually be devoted to me, not just to his stomach.

I don't get a newspaper delivered to my house, so I was a bit surprised when, during a Sunday morning meditation, my spirit told me to look in the classified section of the LA Times. When I asked why, She told me that "my puppy" was advertised there. My spirit said that my puppy was a female, black standard poodle (one of the breeds that I was considering), and that she was very intuitive. I went out and bought the paper, and sure enough the classifieds contained exactly one advertisement for standard poodle puppies. There were three puppies available—two males and a female—and when I first held the female, I could feel that she already belonged to me. I don't know how else to describe that feeling of "coming home," but once you've felt it, you know not to settle for anything less. That was how Lola came into my life.

My spirit was so right about her being intuitive! From the time she was a puppy, Lola could read a dog's body language faster and more accurately than I could, and I'm an animal behaviorist *and* an intuitive! When I've held meditation classes in my home, Lola has always curled up at the feet of the person who was the most ill or the most troubled. When a client enters the house with lots of negative energy and drama around her, Lola doesn't approach her until she's had a session and is more balanced. She's the best dog that I've ever had, and I'm grateful to the Universe for matching us up together.

But I digress, I was telling you about Dr. Stevenson.

Dr. Ann Stevenson is a caring, dedicated doctor who comes to see me in order to do everything she can for her patients. She arrives with a list of patients that she has questions about, and as she pictures each person in her mind, I can connect with Ann's spirit and receive information about that patient. Usually I hear her spirit tell me about emotional factors that are contributing to the patient's symptoms since this is the primary focus of my work. But sometimes I'm also given medical information, such as the best combination of medicines to use, a symptom that the patient forgot to mention, or additional tests that should be run.

Ann is a doctor that warrants respect. She graduated at the top of her class from an Ivy League college and medical school and stays abreast of current research in standard Western medicine and complementary medicine. She's a very skillful doctor and very compassionate. The only difficulty that I see in Ann's life now is that she's infatuated with one of her yoga instructors named Doug.

I believe that some male yoga instructors today are like the tennis pros of the 70s and 80s—real *players* who enjoy flirting with women and making them feel attractive. Ann knows this but finds herself weak in the knees when her teacher approaches her to correct her yoga postures. She's been married for twelve years and still loves her husband but has spent more than one session asking her spirit about her fascination with Doug.

I opened the door to see Ann dressed in yoga clothes, with her energy looking frazzled and "stirred-up." Since this is not how a person typically looks (energetically) after a yoga class, I concluded that Doug was her yoga instructor today. Ann plopped down on the sofa in my treatment room and immediately got to work. She brought out a short stack of patient files. Each one had a sticky note on the front of it with the question that she wanted me to ask her spirit.

"Bethany Simpson, aged 25, suffering from migraine headaches," she quickly rattled off. "She's been tested for food allergies—has none—and doesn't seem to have a lot of stress right now. I'm suspecting a hormonal imbalance since the headaches occur at fairly regular intervals, and I'm thinking of starting her on birth control pills, which she's wanting anyway." Ann's spirit confirmed that this was the approach that would likely bring about the fastest result and said that Bethany's hormones and periods had always been rather irregular. "Yes, that's true," Ann confirmed. I asked Ann to offer some names of the birth control pills she was considering, and Ann's spirit suggested one that would be the easiest for Bethany's body to work with. Her spirit also mentioned that Bethany drank red wine frequently, and that the sulfites used to make the wine caused her body to be more prone to headaches. Until the birth control pills regulated her hormones and made her less prone to migraines, Bethany was advised to avoid red wine.

Next Ann asked her spirit about a patient who needed diagnostic tests in order to determine what was causing her painful symptoms. There were three tests that could be ordered, all of which would be expensive and unpleasant for the patient. Ann's spirit suggested the order that She recommended Ann do the tests. In the past when Ann has gotten such a list, she has typically received the information that she needed from the first test and never needed to run the other tests. In this case, a particular test was recommended, and Ann's spirit also offered insight into something happening in this patient's personal life that was contributing to her condition.

Ann asked questions about two more patients, and then we turned our focus to Ann's personal life. "Okay...," she began. "I know I sound like a broken record, but what is up with me and this yoga instructor?! I find myself thinking about him and planning what I'll wear to yoga class, and in general, acting like some silly school girl with a crush! I know that I'm not thinking of running off with this guy—he's ten years younger than me and probably makes less than half of my income—but why am I so obsessed with him?"

Ann's spirit asked her what Doug offered that was different than what her husband, Tom, offered. "Well, Tom is a great guy—very responsible, honest, a good provider, and a hard worker, but he's, you know...kind of stodgy. He goes to work, comes home, and turns on the TV to watch sports and unwind. I know that he loves me a lot, but he isn't passionate or even that affectionate. Doug is sensitive and spiritual and notices every little detail about me. He likes to read poetry out loud to the class to help us feel more connected to our hearts. And when he talks to me, his energy just flows over me and I feel...special. Like some of that passion that he has for life has just surged into me."

Ann's spirit observed, "*It sounds like you feel that you have to choose either a passionate lover or a responsible man.*"

"Yes!" exclaimed Ann. "That's one way of describing it. Doug's more in the category of 'starving artist,' and Tom's more like 'good husband material'."

"*Why do you feel that you must choose?*" her spirit asked. "*Most people get trapped into thinking in these terms, believing that they must have either stability in their partner or passion and a deep emotional connection. But if you believe that you cannot have both within one relationship, then you will not look for it, and you will not experience it.*"

Ann looked like she was rising to a challenge. "Are you telling me that if I just look for those qualities in Tom then 'Poof!' they will suddenly be there? Because I don't think so."

"*No,*" her spirit answered patiently. "*I'm saying that if we don't expect a person to possess certain qualities, then we don't nurture that side of the relationship, and consequently the relationship includes very little of those elements. But nearly everyone possesses the qualities of passion and emotional intimacy. For some men, these qualities were nurtured during their childhood. For others, such qualities must be cultivated during their adulthood.*

"*But most women are taught to see their man as some sort of statue, carved in stone and unchanging. Humans expect their children to change tremendously over a ten-year period but expect adults to remain relatively unaltered over the same decade. This presumption encourages people to stagnate in their personal development once they stop attending school, and this is unfortunate and unnecessary. Please don't assume that Tom has no interest in developing additional aspects to your relationship with him."*

Ann thought for a moment. "Okay, I hear what my spirit is saying. But I still don't see Tom ever reading poetry to me. So what does my spirit suggest as a way to move him—and us—in the direction I want to go in? In other words, how do I compete with the sports channel? Should I disconnect our satellite dish?"

Ann's spirit was quick to answer. *"Try to refrain from doing battle in any way. Do not think that you have to compete with the television or any activity in Tom's life. When you first fell in love, did you feel like you had to compete with sports for Tom's attention?"*

"No, not at all. But that was a million years ago, when we were both young and discovering each other's bodies!"

"It was also because Tom had been conditioned by your culture to expect to act differently when he fell in love. He gave himself permission to feel more passion, to explore emotional intimacy with you, and to stay more connected to his emotions during that time. This same culture taught him to expect that passion to die down and be replaced by stability and the comfort of predictability. But these categories need not be so starkly different from each other. When people in a relationship begin to miss some of the exciting portions of a relationship, they mistakenly assume that they must start a new relationship in order to experience those portions again. It is—"

"I'm not going to have an affair with Doug," Ann

interrupted. "I just want to stop yearning for him or for someone like him."

Her spirit continued, *"Yes, and your truth is that you want to feel more of these feelings for your husband, not Doug."*

"Yes!" Ann said with an exasperated look on her face.

"Then I ask you to hear the rest of this suggestion. Choose one quality at a time that you would like to experience more of in your marriage then begin holding the intent to include it in your relationship. Look for it, encourage it, and reinforce it. I will help you to begin. You mentioned that Doug notices little things, as if he is focused on you intently. My suggestion is to propose to your husband that you begin having a weekend away once a month. For the first getaway, ask him to plan every aspect of the weekend, including where you stay and which restaurants you eat in. Since he knows the location of your trip, he will need to advise you as to which clothes to pack."

"What?! Tom doesn't even know the phone numbers of the restaurants we usually go to. I handle all those reservations and details. He wouldn't know where to begin, and it might aggravate him if I dump that all on him."

"He manages to handle all the specific features involved in his job, doesn't he? You may be surprised by his attention to detail. After all, he's able to focus on complex issues at work, isn't he?"

"Well...yes," Ann agreed.

"Then I recommend that you try this idea," Ann's spirit said. *"An arrangement such as this asks him to focus on you in a way that is different than how you currently interact. And this sort of change is healthy*

*for a relationship—it helps prevent it from feeling
stale. And the next getaway will be yours to plan."*

As Ann thought about the idea, she glowed with
anticipation and then began to tear up. "I just
realized that I haven't paid attention to those sort
of details with Tom either. I'm so busy noticing how
he's not romancing me that I'm ignoring how I've
fallen into my own self-involved patterns. Okay! I'm
going to do it—tell my spirit thanks!"

I gave Ann an energy treatment, but the session
had already smoothed down her energy and balanced
her chakras so that there was not much that needed
my attention. Ann looked more radiant and felt
optimistic and empowered as she left my treatment
room. Another great day at the office! I love my job.

Follow-up:

I'm happy to report that Ann and her husband
enjoyed a fabulous weekend getaway to Lake Tahoe.
Her husband forgot a few small details (like forgetting
to pack socks for himself), but they problem-solved
easily together and had a wonderful adventure. The
next month they were committed to attending a
wedding and several other events, so they waited
until the following month to go on another getaway
that Ann planned. She found that she enjoyed the
slight bit of stress involved in organizing the details
and surprising her husband, and their trip to Palm
Springs was equally successful.

Ann has commented more than once that she is
surprised by how quickly her infatuation with Doug
has faded.

Chapter 6

Dating Observations

It's another beautiful day here in southern California. It's also another day of me yelling and rushing the kids out the door so that they're not late for school. As a student of Buddhism for many years, I really value and treasure calm, serene energy. But that is rarely the energy in my house on school mornings. As peaceful as I may appear to my clients when I'm lecturing or in session, school mornings seem to be the universal equalizer for all of us. I don't care if you're a movie star or a prominent politician, your kids will push you to the brink of insanity most mornings as they meander around the house in no apparent hurry to get to school on time. Over the years I've learned to schedule my client sessions to begin at 10 a.m., knowing that I need time to get the kids in the car, drop them off at school, exhale the frustration out of my body as I drive to the park, and then exercise to fully decompress. My kids are old enough to drive now, and my oldest son, Joey, has his own car to drive himself and his brother to high school. But they still seem to require me to cajole them into the shower, then downstairs to eat, then upstairs to brush their teeth, etc.

This morning brings an added twist. Joey's car is in the shop, so we pile into my car so that I can drop the boys off. As we pull up to the school, Joey covers one eye with his right hand. "Hmmm," he says. "I think I forgot to put my contacts in. I can't see anything. Mom, can you go home and get them for me? I can't be late for class because I have a test today."

"Are you kidding me?!" I storm. "Didn't you notice that you couldn't see a damn thing the whole ride to school?"

"Uh, no...I guess I wasn't paying attention." Spoken like a true teenager.

I tell the kids to get out of the car (Where is that eject button when I want one? It would feel so good to hit that today!), and I race back to the house to get Joey's contact lenses and drop them off at the school office. I drive like one of those crazed soccer moms I resent, the ones who plaster their SUV with bumper stickers proclaiming their love of their honor-roll student, but who are willing to endanger everyone else's honor-roll students by driving through their neighborhoods at double the speed limit. I'm sure that living with a mom who is an intuitive is often a unique experience for my kids, but we sure have plenty of "normal" moments too.

I get to the park a few minutes ahead of my friend and have to convince my dog to stand in the parking lot and wait while the rolling green lawn of the park beckons her. Part of my reason for buying a large dog, even though I live in a house with a tiny yard, is that I know that I don't have the self-discipline needed to get out of bed and exercise before work. But I can't imagine looking into this loyal dog's big brown eyes and asking her to go without exercise when I know how blissfully happy it makes her to run in the park. So I set myself up to exercise regularly by using guilt as my motivator (can you tell I had some Catholic teachings in my childhood?). Which is why we are here, waiting for my friend Maggie.

Maggie lives in my neighborhood and works for a movie distribution company in Los Angeles. Because she's able to work from home some of the time, we power walk or run together a couple of mornings each week. Maggie's bright, quirky, and funny, and it's an easy, comfortable friendship.

Maggie is single and has never had kids. She goes through periods of dating and then periods of avoiding men, depending on how she feels about her body, her life, and love in general. She's the person who gave me the inside scoop on how to date online, with valuable tips like: meet for coffee so if he's boring you're not stuck for an entire two hour dinner, and Google him to see if he's being honest about his age and occupation. She is much bolder than I am. Example: Last year she arranged to meet a guy at a local coffee shop for a first date. She had liked his photos and enjoyed talking to him on the phone. She got to the coffee shop early and took a seat facing the door so that she could see him as he walked in. When he arrived, she could see that he looked almost nothing like his photos, which were probably taken fifteen years earlier. She got up, tossed her coffee cup in the trash can, and walked right past him and out the door. As she brushed past him she said, "No way. I won't waste your time, and I wish that you hadn't wasted mine. I won't date someone who starts off with dishonesty. Get new pictures on your profile!" The guy just stood there with is mouth open. I'm sure it was the shortest date he's ever had.

This morning Maggie got out of the car wearing a cute pair of yoga pants and a coordinating top. I glanced down at my sloppy clothes and reminded myself that I'm not just dressing for my dog, but that other people see me in this park too. Oh well, Maggie didn't seem to notice as she fell into step beside me and patted Lola on the head before the dog streaked off across the grass after some insolent squirrel who had dared to enter her park uninvited.

"So what happened last night?" I asked. Maggie had been set up on a date by her dental hygienist. My dental hygienist offers no such gems when she cleans my teeth. I leave there with nothing more than a travel toothbrush and a package of dental floss. I've heard that my hygienist recently got engaged to another dentist, so clearly she's been holding out on some leads on available men. Note to self: Shop for new hygienist.

Maggie took a deep breath. "Well...it was interesting. He was cute—nice eyes and a good body—you know I can't take a guy seriously who doesn't take his own body maintenance seriously."

"Yes, yes," I said, urging her along. "So what's the catch? I can tell by your voice that there's a catch here."

"Well, he's Jewish."

"So?"

"Well, he gets all this pressure from his family to settle down with a nice Jewish girl, but he seems open to dating women who aren't Jewish."

"That's good, 'cause last time I checked you weren't Jewish," I said smiling.

Maggie continued. "We hit it off, but I felt like he was hinting around at this idea of me being willing to lie to his family and tell them that I was Jewish. Or entertain the idea of converting."

"You covered this on a first date?!" I was incredulous. "How about getting to know him before you start talking about converting to a new religion so you can please the family?"

Maggie stopped walking and looked at me with a serious expression on her face. "Christine, I'm not getting any younger. I'm single in a town where it's fine for successful 60-year-old men to date 29-year-old actresses, but successful 60-year-old women can typically *not* date 29-year-old guys. So maybe sometimes you have to make concessions."

I felt a wave of compassion for Maggie because I knew where she was coming from in that moment. Most women have this fear of not being able to find a great guy, and the more birthdays we have, the stronger the fear seems to get. On most days Maggie and I stay out of this quicksand of negative thought, but we each slide into it now and then.

"Maggie, you're just feeling scarcity right now, like there aren't enough great men out there. I get that, but you don't want to make decisions from this place. And you're not interested in Judaism are you? Would that be a religion that you would choose to study if it weren't for this guy?"

"No," she exhaled as we walked up a hill. "I mean, I have no strong feelings against it, but I'm kind of like you—a student of Buddhism and Taoism and quite happy not to have to wear any one label."

"And another thing," I continued, on a roll now. "You've been telling me lately how the books that you've been reading have focused on integrity and living from your authentic self. How does this idea align with that?"

"It doesn't," she groaned. "And I guess it can't be creating good karma for me to fake a religious belief can it?"

"It doesn't feel like your highest move," I agreed. "But if we take the religion out of the picture, how did you feel about the guy?"

"Now that I'm talking to you, I can see that I was looking for how it could all work, you know? Like I was going down a shopping list and saying in my head: good body, check; good job, check; decent sense of humor, check. But in actuality, there wasn't any chemistry there."

"Maybe that's because you were both comparing each other to your inventory lists instead of actually feeling who was in front of you," I offered. "Is it worth a second date to just be present with him and see?"

"No," Maggie said disappointedly. "If I'm honest with myself, I have to admit that he didn't really excite me. He was nice enough but kind of boring. And his willingness to ask a woman to lie in order to please his mother is a big turnoff."

"Yeah, I get that," I agreed. "So let's just throw that one back in the ocean and trust that there's a better match out there for you."

"Yeah, I guess so," Maggie sighed.

"I think that this is the downside of first dates," I said gently. "If the date doesn't work out, then people seem to feel more alone than they did before the date. When the guy turns out to be uninteresting, it's as if the woman just received more evidence that there really isn't a good match out there for her. And then she has to work hard to gear herself up to go out on another first date."

"But what's the alternative?" Maggie asked sadly. "Never go out on a first date because then you won't ever be disappointed? Then you'll definitely be alone forever!"

"No, I think the answer is to have a different approach to first dates," I replied. "I try to look at them as a chance to meet interesting people and hear their stories. You know, how they got to be at this place in their life. I think that people are fascinating. And if I approach the first date as a chance to meet someone new and hear his story, then I don't apply that mental checklist through the whole date, trying to see if he matches what I'm looking for. Does that make sense?"

"Yeah," Maggie said, "it does. I know that I have to stay away from that fear-based thinking that has me worrying that I'll never find someone."

"Yes," I agreed. "Because if that fear is driving you, then each date carries the burden of having to rescue you from that terrible fate of being alone forever. And that's too much pressure to put onto a first meeting. But the kicker is, I don't really have fears of living alone forever. I love my alone time—so much so that I get nervous about eventually living with someone and having to give it up."

Maggie grinned. "You probably don't have a fear of ending up alone because you have kids. Because from what I see nowadays, kids never leave their parents' house for long. So maybe you already know that you'll never really be alone for long."

"That's true," I laughed. "Kids now seem to boomerang back home at least once. When I think about it, I'm open to living with a man, but I can also be happy living alone and getting together with someone several nights a week. Do I sound like someone who's going to end up living with ten cats?"

"No, you sound like a bachelor," Maggie said, "and I don't know if I'm impressed or disappointed. I know that I definitely want to live with someone. I want to wake up next to the guy I love and know that we're going to grow old together. And it's my fear of not finding him that sends me into these moments of scarcity thinking."

"I get that," I conceded, "but we both know that thoughts create, so I think that we can help keep each other out of the quicksand of any kind of scarcity thinking. Because when you go to that fearful place of 'Oh no, there aren't any good men out there,' then that's all you're going to experience, right? So let's focus on the good men that we have met and remember that there are hundreds, if not thousands, of men that we will meet in our future. If we stay positive, then we will put out the vibrations to attract the best possible matches for each of us. Agreed?"

"Agreed," said Maggie, and just then I could have sworn that Lola looked up at us and winked, adding her own canine approval of our pact.

Chapter 7

What I Perceive

To help explain how I perceive the connection between thoughts and emotions and what shows up in the body, I'd like to share with you some of what I perceive, and what I understand about energy.

Every living thing runs on energy, and humans continuously draw in energy and discharge it out of their bodies. There are different ways of examining this energy and its contribution to the body's functioning. EKG machines measure how the energy in the heart area fuels the heart so it can pump blood throughout the body. Acupuncturists feel the energy moving through pulse points in the wrist to gauge how well the energetic pathways are carrying energy to various organs. And some people—like me—can see energy and perceive information about someone's physical and emotional health.

When I look at a client, I can choose to observe her in the standard way, using my senses to see her clothes, smell her perfume, and hear her voice.

Or I can shift my focus and perceive her energy. Just as can you shift your perception to notice the color of someone's eyes instead of listening to what she's saying, I can shift my perception to observe a person's energy.

Even though I refer to this as "seeing someone's energy," that's actually a misnomer; it's actually more of a multi-sensory experience. If I'm calm and focused on another person, I can see colors in her energy field, and when she speaks, I can sense her energy moving in ways that indicate certain patterns of thinking, frequently held emotions, etc.

While I'm watching the energy move, I may also be picking up distinctive smells that a client's spirit sends me. For instance, there's an odor, similar to the smell of rotting meat, that I notice when a client has too much animal protein in her diet. Or the smell of cigarette smoke that I notice in people who have compromised lung functioning (even if they don't smoke). By sending me information in multiple ways, the spirit world efficiently conveys large amounts of information to me in seconds.

I now understand that I'm not shown everything that is happening in a person's body. There's simply too much going on at once, and I could not register all that data. I'm not even shown all the areas of the person's body that are in need of healing. I'm given information in two categories: items that the client asks about and items that the client's spirit wants addressed.

My job is to expand my client's current awareness. So as a client begins speaking about her stomach and how it hurts when she attends family functions,

I'll first receive information about any physical causes of the stomach aches, and then I'll be given information about the emotional causes. As the client begins discussing her family dynamics, her energy reveals when she's empowered, when she's unsure, and when she's confused. And when she mentions one family member in particular and the energy in her stomach area turns black, I know that her spirit is showing me the heart of the issue. Then I stop and channel, asking her spirit for details about how the client can resolve the underlying issue.

Over the years I've seen thousands of clients, each with physical symptoms that correlate to how they internalize the stress in their lives. Different areas of the body seem to correspond to particular subjects or ideas. When we feel stress, we produce negative thoughts and emotions, which is negative energy. This negative energy seems to settle into the area of the body that corresponds to the subject. So a client who comes to see me complaining of frequent throat issues is probably storing a lot of her stress in that area of the body, creating a "weak area." From my spirit (and many others), I've learned that the throat area represents one's ability to speak her truth without fear of repercussions or being ignored. So a complete healing of her symptoms will include helping the client see when she holds herself back from speaking freely and what "punishment" she is afraid of experiencing when she is honest. Each time she has fearful thoughts about speaking her truth, she produces negative energy in this area of her body, further weakening the area by interfering with normal cell functioning.

This explains something that has always confused me. There are many conditions and symptoms that cause doctors to proclaim, "Stress will make your condition worse." But why do different types of stress seem to aggravate different symptoms? When I'm nervous about an upcoming event that I must speak in, my stomach has difficulty digesting rich foods. But such stress doesn't seem to affect my lower back—that gets tight when I'm worried about money. The answer is that each of my fears leads me to create and store stress in a different part of my body.

Understanding the issues related to each area of the body can help us to understand how our bodies are always giving us feedback, registering the quantity of negative thoughts that we're producing and in which subject areas. This is why I suggest that people view their symptoms like text messages being sent from their spirit. Your body is being used like a cell phone with messages that pop up day and night in order to get your attention. These symptoms/messages are lovingly sent to you in order to help you notice and resolve stressful issues so that you can feel more content.

In the Appendix, I've provided a list of some of the most common patterns that I see—the physical symptom and the most frequent emotional issue underneath it. Many symptoms are not included in the appendix because there are several possible emotional messages that may be contributing to that type of symptom. After each listed symptom, there are questions to help you identify the internal conflicts that may be causing your condition. Relating to your body and your symptoms in this way can help you more accurately identify how you are internalizing the stress in your life.

Chapter 8

Carolyn's Follow-Up Session – Embracing Change

Carolyn was on time for her session and wearing a big smile.

"Things are better at home and with my body!" she announced proudly when I opened the front door.

"That's wonderful!" I beamed back at her as I led her into the treatment room.

Carolyn reported that at first when she tried to speak to her husband, he'd gotten defensive, but this time she hadn't backed away when he reacted negatively. Instead she reminded herself that avoiding confrontation was less important than being heard and accomplishing a change in her household. She kept talking, and eventually her husband heard what she was saying. Carolyn's spirit asked what changes she had noticed.

"Well, he's making more of an effort to help around the house and to be more engaged with us. It just feels more positive in our home now. My digestion is so much better, and even the fatigue is better.

But there hasn't really been much improvement in my eczema."

I connected to Carolyn's spirit who offered an explanation for the eczema.

"Your skin is still inflamed because now you're allowing many different things to 'get under your skin.' You've given yourself permission to notice and discuss what is unsatisfactory to you, which is very good. But like a pendulum, you have swung too far in the other direction, as if you need to compensate for how out of balance things have been."

"Oh no! She's right! I am doing that. The kids have complained that I'm picking on them and nagging them to help out around the house. Because I see that I was doing everything, I want to hand over chores to the kids and to Bill so that I can lighten my load. And I don't feel guilty about it! I really see that how we were living was unfair to me."

Carolyn's spirit agreed. *"Your redistribution of the workload is very healthy, but it's recommended that you don't try to fix everything at once. Try not to have resentment for how things were in the past. Everyone was living in the way that they thought would bring them the most happiness. Now that you know better, you can live differently, but you will cause new suffering if you hold resentment over your past actions and those of your family members."*

"That sounds like such good advice," said Carolyn, "but I can't help but feel a sense of urgency to make this all right."

"And can you define 'right'?"

"You know—where everything is in balance, and we're each doing the amount of work that's fair."

"I would suggest that what is in balance and fair for your family will change from day to day and week to week, depending on the needs of each of you. Do you agree?"

"Yes," Carolyn agreed. "But I still want to get us at least a bit closer to being in balance!"

"Can you feel the resentment in your body that I mentioned a moment ago?"

"Yeah, I guess I can." Carolyn looked sheepish.

"Please talk about those feelings for a moment," requested Carolyn's spirit.

"Well, my first thought is that I'm frustrated at the kids and Bill for taking advantage of me. But then my next thought is that they were treating me just how I allowed them to treat me. So that leaves me...mad at myself. Mad because I didn't see it sooner. How I was running myself ragged to try and be the perfect mom, wife, and employee, and that it was killing me and it was never going to change."

"Humans are the only species that learn something and then feel anger towards themselves once they've learned it—anger that they didn't already know it. As if life is not meant to be experienced but figured out before one arrives. Since it is impossible to know the best action to take in every foreseeable situation, I recommend that you avoid needless suffering by having compassion for yourself after you learn something."

"Wow! I never thought of it that way before. You're right—I'm frustrated at myself for 'doing it wrong' for so many years, and so now I'm riding everyone so hard because I'm trying to make up for lost time. As if I can somehow erase the past by getting everyone to live really balanced now." Carolyn laughed at herself, and her energy softened.

"*Another note of caution,*" offered her spirit. "*Since Bill has appeared to agree with your assessment of him as needing to engage with the family more, you've helped him to take on some shame about his past behavior. This also serves no purpose, and does not help him live as the empowered man that you spoke of missing during your first session. If you make the space for Bill to forgive himself, then he can more fully embody the energy that he used to have with your family. Again, the idea is to learn and then move forward happily, with no punishment for not already possessing knowledge.*"

"Guilty as charged—again!" Carolyn said, then looked exasperated with herself. "I'm surprised that I'm feeling as healthy as I am considering the mistakes that I've been making."

Carolyn's spirit jumped in, "*Please be clear that you've made significant progress in honoring yourself and therefore in honoring all of the people that you're in a relationship with. These suggestions and observations do not alter that. I am explaining why your skin is still inflamed. The cause of your inflammation has shifted, but this shift is in the right direction. Previously your inflammation was about a situation that you were not even aware of. Now you are actively seeking a more balanced life, and the inflammation is due to self-blame and impatience. Changing these patterns of thought will be beneficial to you in many other ways, in addition to helping your eczema.*"

"Well, that's good news," Carolyn sighed in relief.

"Sometimes it's helpful to picture a young child in second grade who is learning math. If the child was taught to feel shame each time she made a mistake, how fast would her learning progress?"

"Not too quickly because she would probably shut down."

"Precisely. And adults tend to resist learning— learning things about themselves and about healthy changes that they could make—because of the ensuing self-judgment. We are more compassionate with children, and we tell them that they are not expected to know everything already—that's why they go to school. But school is not capable of teaching a person everything that she will need to know throughout her entire life, agreed?"

Carolyn nodded. "Yes, that's definitely true. It'd be impossible to teach a kid everything he needed to learn to make every decision for the rest of his life."

"Yes! And yet adults tend to judge themselves when they have to learn through the process of 'getting it wrong.' This self-judgment implies that no more learning should be necessary beyond a certain age."

"Well, okay. When you phrase it like that, we all sound ridiculous."

"No, just hard on yourselves due to unrealistic expectations that you're not even aware of. The point of this conversation is to make you aware of the expectations that you hold unconsciously so that you can intentionally decide if you want to keep those expectations and standards for yourself."

"No, I definitely don't. But I don't think that this will be quick and easy to change."

"True. You will need to watch yourself, paying attention to when you feel self-judgment of any kind. When you do, ask why you're feeling frustrated with yourself. The idea is to raise your awareness so that over time you break this unproductive habit of self-loathing. Along the way you may spot other habits of thought, patterns of negative thinking that you've done for years but not really examined. Questioning your negative thoughts is the best way to sort out which ones actually help you move forward and which ones impede joyful living."

"Interesting. I guess that a lot of the self-criticism that I do happens because I think that somehow I will be less prone to make similar mistakes in the future if I beat myself up about the ones I've already made."

"And again I will direct you back to the analogy of a child learning math. If you continually remind her of the mistake that she made on the first day of learning a new computation and cause her to feel guilty about it, is this the best way to help her avoid repeating that mistake?"

Carolyn laughed. "Well, I want to say yes, but I'm guessing that that's not the right answer, so because I want to get it correct, I'll say no."

"I appreciate your honesty and this is a common misperception. But it's not shame that makes a child strive to do better—it is the search for praise and self-love. While it's true that guilt and shame will coerce a child to avoid some behaviors, overall learning thrives in an environment where successes are praised and mistakes are handled with compassion and an understanding that this is part

of the learning process."

"Boy, I sure wish that my school had approached learning that way," Carolyn sighed.

"But you are still in school because throughout your life you will always be learning. Only now you are in charge of how mistakes are handled. So decide on the most compassionate, effective learning policy, and then employ it on yourself. Changing how you speak to yourself internally will take some time, but it will increase your feelings of inner tranquility immensely and increase your enthusiasm about learning new things—about yourself and others."

Carolyn smiled. "That makes sense. Okay, I'm in! I'll start trying to notice how I'm talking to myself throughout each day. And I'll try to go easier on myself and my family."

I gave Carolyn an energy treatment to help her eczema calm down and recommended that she use the homeopathic remedy Sulphur, which is very helpful in treating eczema. As she left, I noticed how much calmer Carolyn felt and how her energy looked less urgent and impatient. I knew that she was off to a good start with her new intentions.

Follow-up:

Over the past year Carolyn has experienced wonderful healing—both physically and emotionally. She has increased her awareness of her own negative self-talk and has learned to disagree with her inner critic. She now holds more reasonable expectations of herself, and when we meet once a month for a session, her spirit helps her see how her increasing reliance on her family members has enabled everyone to feel empowered.

Bill now works part-time for his former employer and part-time as a freelance photographer. He hopes to work full-time as a photographer within the next year but holds himself responsible for earning the income that he has promised to contribute. Their marriage feels more like it did prior to Bill losing his job, and both of them are committed to maintaining the more honest communication that they are enjoying.

Carolyn's fatigue is gone, but a minor version of her digestive issues resurfaces occasionally when she slips back into old patterns of negative self-talk. Her eczema is healed because at the first sign of itching, Carolyn stops to notice what resentments may be building up within her. In short, her symptoms are essentially gone, requiring no medications of any kind. Carolyn is calmer, more empowered, and enjoying her excellent health.

Chapter 9

―――⦿―――

Hardening the Heart/Opening the Heart

Maggie was walking and talking fast this morning and gesturing too. I suspected that she'd already had her two cups of coffee. She was sharing an "ah-ha" moment that she'd had that morning in the shower.

"The other day you made a comment that maybe I approach every first date as if I'm speed dating. You know, like I'm only giving each guy thirty seconds to prove that he's not totally wrong for me before I write him off. And I realized that you're right! I'm so convinced that I'm going to be disappointed that I barely invest any of myself when I meet someone."

I tried to empathize. "That doesn't sound like much fun—for you or the guy!"

Maggie nodded. "But there's more to it than that—I realize that I hold myself back in *every* way, even after the first date. Even when I've been in a relationship, I haven't made myself as vulnerable emotionally, and I haven't shared as much of myself as I used to. That way if things don't work out, I won't get as hurt."

"I hear you, but I wonder if that plan ever works. I know that by the time someone's in her 30s or 40s, they've had plenty of heartache from relationships ending, and the easiest thing to do is to harden their heart."

Maggie looked at me with raised eyebrows. "Harden their heart?"

"Yeah. Shut it down, close off—do what you were talking about where you make yourself less vulnerable by sharing less of yourself so you can minimize your pain if the relationship ends. I don't think that this *actually does* lessen any potential pain, but I think that people do it anyway. Most people get more cynical and less romantic in an attempt to manage any future disappointment."

"You're right!" Maggie agreed. "That's what I'm doing—managing potential future disappointment. And not doing a very good job at it, I might add."

"But I don't think you *can* do a good job of it because I think that it's impossible. I mean, how can you avoid being disappointed when a relationship doesn't work out? So since you can't avoid disappointment—it's part of the deal with relationships—what are you missing out on when you do try to minimize that disappointment?

Maggie's shoulders drooped. "I think you miss out on everything. The physical passion, the emotional excitement, the curiosity about getting to know someone new—all of it. But why do we keep our hearts shut down once we know that it cuts us off from all the good stuff too?"

I thought a moment. "My spirit has told me that

our egos will keep track of the hurtful stuff to try to protect us from going through something like that again."

"As if you ever experience the exact same emotional pain twice," scoffed Maggie.

"Right, but I think that we all keep score anyway, keeping a tally of every bad breakup, every infidelity, etc. But we don't bother to keep track of the good stuff—we figure that we don't need to since we don't have to be on the lookout to avoid it in the future. This means that we're keeping this running list of what can go wrong, but not a list of what can go right."

"Yeah, because we're not trying to prevent things from going well!" Maggie agreed.

"But that leaves people keeping track of the bad stuff much more than the good stuff, which gives them a distorted view of love and relationships. The result is the bitterness that so many people seem to feel about love, and the closing down of the heart that we're talking about."

"Very good, Dr. Freud!" said Maggie. "Now what do we do about it?"

"I think we should each challenge ourselves to have emotional courage. I teach my clients that we incarnate in order to experience love and loss, joy and sorrow—all of it, not just the good stuff. I think it's common to get upset when we experience an emotion that we don't enjoy, but let's face it, do any of us go to see movies that are 100% positive?"

"No, I guess not...," Maggie said.

"Exactly! Because we want to feel moved, and we want to visit both ends of the emotional spectrum.

Watching a character experience success feels better if he's had some struggle and heartache first right?"

"Yeah, I guess so," Maggie agreed reluctantly.

"Heck, even kids' movies have conflict and loss in them, something for the hero to work through and recover from. I remember tearing up watching *The Lion King* movie because the baby lion's father dies! And when the cub is triumphant later, we feel rejuvenated by his success and happiness. My spirit says that each spirit also wants to have a full experience. They want to ride the whole the emotional roller coaster that we each experience in a lifetime.

"But we all seem to get lulled into this entitled way of thinking, believing that since we're trying to make good choices that we are somehow due a pain-free life. Then we respond to each unpleasant experience with resentment."

"Wow! You're so right! And your spirit is so right—you're both smart. So what's the solution? I don't think I can suddenly start being grateful for the painful moments of my life."

"I understand," I said, smiling. "But one way to reverse the ego's tendency to only keep lists of what can go wrong is to focus more on what can go right. Recall some of the positive experiences that you've had in past relationships. If relationships caused nothing but pain then people wouldn't keep searching for them, right? So make your ego keep a more balanced score sheet. That's one of the benefits of gratitude journals. My clients who keep those journals are almost always my happiest clients. Not because their lives are so much better, but because they keep things in better perspective. They're aware of the things that go wrong and are equally aware of the things that go right."

Maggie smiled brightly. "Okay, I'm with ya! Let's do a little reminiscing about some of our great love relationships."

We spent the remainder of our walk reliving fun, romantic moments from our past. It was wonderful, and I thought of loving scenes that hadn't run through my mind in twenty years. Before we got into our cars, we both commented on how great it felt to talk positively about loving relationships instead of dwelling on past disappointments and hurts. Maggie's energy was glowing, and her heart chakra was wide open. I took a moment to bask in a feeling of gratitude I had for all my past loves.

As I loaded Lola in the car, I said to Maggie, "I liked hearing your great stories. They didn't make me laugh as hard as some of the funny dating stories that you've shared, but they sure did make me smile."

Maggie grinned mischievously. "I think that you owe *me* a funny dating story. Your dates seem to go pretty smoothly compared to mine."

"Oh no, I definitely have some strange and funny stories in my history. Like the guy who almost got his car stolen during our date."

"Oh? Do tell!" Maggie enthused.

"That's a long, embarrassing story and we're at the end of the walk, so I'll save it for tomorrow."

Chapter 10

My Strangest Date

The next morning Maggie was at the park waiting for me as I pulled in. As I opened my car door, she looked expectant.

"Okay, I've waited patiently for twenty-four hours. Let's hear your embarrassing date story!" she insisted.

"Oh God, I was hoping you'd forget about that!" I groaned.

"No way!" she laughed. "Clearly I'm short on entertainment these days, so c'mon—spill it!"

As we started walking, I took a deep breath. "Okay, so meeting interesting single men can be a challenge, right?"

"Yes, yes," she agreed impatiently.

"Since I run my practice out of my home, I can go for long stretches without meeting any single, attractive men. So I decided to try internet dating, especially after hearing Karin talk about how she met her fiancé that way."

Maggie kept quiet but nodded her head quickly

as if to prod the story along.

"Well, first I noticed that I became sort of addicted—I spent way too much time 'shopping' for men and responding to all the other shoppers who were also practicing gluttony."

Maggie chuckled. "Well that's just like your personality—intense. You go after things full force and then sometimes burn out quickly. We're like the tortoise and the hare. When I tried internet dating, I used it like a swimming pool; I dipped in for a short time, got cooled off, and then got back out. Although I guess that can also be called 'being a chicken'!"

"Well at least you're the tortoise—he won the race in the end! Hmm...what does that mean for me?"

Maggie refocused the conversation. "Don't get side-tracked—back to the story!"

"Okay, okay. His name was Dan—I think—I've tried to block this all out. We met online, and he was witty and cute, and I agreed to meet him for lunch in Malibu. We were eating at that cute bistro near the movie theater—the one that has an outside eating area—and other than the birds that kept landing near us to scavenge for scraps, it was very pleasant. When Dan asked for more details about my work, I wanted to be honest but reveal things gradually. So I started by saying that doctors referred patients to me to help the patients understand how their stress was contributing to their symptoms. Dan was nodding his head and asking intelligent questions, and I was feeling pretty optimistic about him.

"Then a bird landed on the edge of our table. Usually they flew off quickly, but this one hopped a few inches closer to me, and it caught my attention. When I looked over at it, it immediately said—telepathically—'Someone's breaking into his car,' and cocked its head towards Dan."

Maggie's eyes opened wide. "Oh no! What did you do?"

"I didn't know what to do! I don't even tell most of my clients that I can pick up messages from animals sometimes, since it's not really the focus of my practice. But here I was, with potentially important information being given to me, and I didn't know what to do."

"Oh God, I don't know what I would have done," Maggie sympathized.

"Well, I first asked the bird, 'Do you know that it's his car?' 'Well he got out of it,' the bird answered dryly. 'Just thought you'd want to know. I've been telling him, but he's not paying attention'."

Maggie laughed heartedly.

"Yeah, I decided to skip trying to explain to the bird that most humans don't know how to register the pictures and messages that animals sometimes send. I didn't have the time for that conversation and this was certainly not the place. So I just nodded to the bird to thank him, and he flew off. When I looked back up at Dan, he was watching me. He raised one eyebrow to ask me why I was staring at this bird, and I quickly ran through my options. The most tempting option was to say nothing and hope that the burglar/thief couldn't get into Dan's car. But that seemed cowardly, and this was a nice guy who deserved to not have his car stolen, so I took the leap."

"Of course you did. That's so you!" exclaimed Maggie. "You're brave. I would have kept my mouth shut and prayed that the thief couldn't break into the guy's car."

"So I took a deep breath and said, 'Um, I think that someone's trying to break into your car'."

"He said, 'What?!' and looked at me in disbelief then stood up and frantically scanned the parking lot looking for his car. 'No, you can't really see my car from here, so you must be seeing someone else's car,' he said with relief as he sat back down. Now, I could have let it go at that, but I was already in the water, so I kept going. 'Look, I know that this sounds crazy, but that bird that was just on our table said that he saw someone trying to break into your car—the car that you got out of, so I think you might want to check it out.' Dan stammered out the beginnings of a few words but didn't finish any of them, and then he got up and ran off towards the parking lot. I stood up and watched him run. As he got near a blue Mercedes, this guy who was bent over the keypad on the driver's door stood up and walked briskly away. Dan walked back to our table with a bewildered look on his face.

"He said 'Well, you were right. I think that that guy was trying to break into my car. He had a briefcase, which he had put down next to the door as if he was coming out of work and had forgotten his key-code number. But...I don't understand. You couldn't really see my car from where you were sitting, and you didn't even know what kind of car I drive'."

I looked over at Maggie, who was listening

intently and grinning at the predicament that I had gotten myself into.

"I was in deep already, so I tried to explain. 'Well, when you're very intuitive, sometimes you just...pick up things from animals. Messages or pictures...sort of. I can't always control it, but the message came from that bird, and he was trying to be helpful, and... Hey, he was right, so it's all good, right?' I didn't sound convincing, even to me, and Dan's eyes had glazed over part of the way through my fumbling explanation. He stood up and tossed two twenty-dollar bills on the table. 'Hey, I really appreciate you saving my car—you and your little bird friend—but this is a bit too weird for me. Sorry.' And he walked (very quickly) back to his car and never looked back."

"Ouch! So much for honesty," Maggie said sympathetically.

"Yeah, but can you blame him?" I asked. "I would run too if a person I met seemed crazy. Like this guy I met for coffee once who'd heard what I did asked me if I had ever met an alien and wanted to know if I believed in the 'probing' that aliens did to people up on their spaceships. I couldn't get away from him fast enough!"

"Yeah, but that's different," Maggie countered. "You're not crazy! You really did hear that message from that bird, and you really can hear people's spirits."

I smiled. "I know, but sometimes I forget how different my normal is compared to everyone else's."

"That's for sure!" Maggie enthused. "Hey, I know! Why don't you have some of your clients set you up with their single friends? They would probably choose people who are open to what you do."

"No, I don't think so. Several of my clients have talked about setting me up, and they haven't suggested men that I think would be a good match for me."

Maggie's eyebrows raised with interest. "Oh? Do tell!"

"My clients mean well, but they seem to assume that the perfect guy for me will be someone who does yoga, meditates, and practices alternative medicine. In other words, a male version of me. The most important skill that makes me good at my job is intuition, which is an ability that arises from one's female energy, right?"

Maggie nodded her head in agreement.

"Well, we all have male and female energy within us, but a man that has the same degree of intuition that I have is usually going to be too "soft" for me. I mean, hey, I was a lawyer before I discovered my abilities, and I still have that streak of take-charge male energy in me that can be triggered if I think things aren't getting handled. So if a man is hesitant and unsure of himself or is very passive in relationships, I usually end up taking over like a steamroller. Then I'm unhappy and so is he.

"Oh, I get that," Maggie offered. "You were raised to be a very strong woman. Let's face it, your mom can be intimidating with how smart and powerful she is. She has a lot of strong energy, and she taught you to stand up for yourself and follow your own internal rules."

"Yeah," I agreed. "Growing up, my impression of

her was someone who had no fear and almost no personal limitations. Later on I realized that she had insecurities just like the rest of us, but when I was young, she seemed unstoppable. Over the years she's created a volunteer organization, helped my dad run his company, and raised seven kids, four of them adopted from Korea. That's a pretty intense role model."

"Definitely!" agreed Maggie. "My mom was tough too, but not as polished and accomplished as yours. And I learned to use a lot of strong male energy too."

"And in school, my teachers and friends encouraged my strong personality and my tendency to be a leader. I didn't even realize that I was suppressing so much of my female energy and favoring my male energy because our culture doesn't teach us to think in those terms."

Maggie stopped walking and looked at me. "I'm just agreeing with you, but it just dawned on me that I have one definition of male and female energy, and you might be using another. How are you defining those?"

We resumed our brisk pace as I continued. "Okay, so here's what I've learned about male and female energy from my spirit and my clients' spirits: Male energy is the energy within us that pushes us forward and makes us proactive. It's the part of us that's logical, action-oriented, strategic, and organized. Our female energy is less concerned with doing and more focused on listening, feeling, and information gathering. This energy is soft and nurturing and is associated with our emotional side, meaning that we rely on our feelings to guide us. Male energy is associated with our mental side, meaning that we rely on our brain to help us make decisions logically. We each have both types of energy within us, and the balance of each is different in each person. I encourage my clients to use their female energy to feel their truth, and then use their male energy to set boundaries based on what they feel is true. Does that make sense?"

"Absolutely!" Maggie said. "And it makes sense why I can't attract the romantic men I want when I'm in a bossy, dominant space. If I'm in my male energy, then what's left for them? Just female energy? And my first husband and I probably fought so often because we both had that same, strong male energy, and I was afraid to be soft and nurturing because then I thought that he wouldn't respect me."

"Exactly!" I agreed. "We've all been raised in a culture that values male energy much more than female energy. Successful people in our country are usually thought of as assertive, competitive, and full of action. Someone who's more intuitive and empathetic may be seen as admirable, but she's generally less respected and less powerful than an aggressive CEO. So women who want to succeed usually end up focusing on their male energy so they can 'make it in the man's world.' When these women come to see me—because they feel dissatisfied with their lives or because of physical ailments—the solution usually includes teaching them to appreciate their female energy so they can access those strengths."

Maggie was nodding in agreement. "And the beautiful part is that so many companies are now trying to teach their staff to be more intuitive and creative, and this means encouraging them to get in touch with their female energy!"

"Exactly," I enthused. "I now see that our deepest wisdom is actually accessed through our intuition, and so people who learn to tap into this become more successful than they were when they were aggressively pursuing their careers using primarily male energy. But I sure didn't know that back when I was a lawyer!"

Maggie looked reflective. "Developing my intuitive abilities meant turning down the volume on my male energy and teaching myself to rely more on my female energy. But that wasn't easy! I worried that people wouldn't take me as seriously."

It was my turn to nod in agreement. "That was a huge shift for me to make too because I saw female energy as weak and not able to command respect. We live in a country where 'might makes right,' and we set our boundaries and enforce them through our male energy. As a lawyer, I was all about setting boundaries—for myself and others—and I liked feeling powerful. Heck, that's why most of us went to law school—to gain more power in the world. Softening myself—even a little—felt like I was volunteering to be taken advantage of or viewed with less respect. It's been a pleasant surprise to discover that I'm actually wiser when I use my female energy."

Maggie smiled. "What I like is that I have better connections with people at work. When I'm using more female energy, I can relate to people better—I focus on understanding their point of view instead of just pushing them to hear mine. In the corporate world, we call it 'developing your EQ'—your emotional quotient."

I thought for a moment. "But since I've had so many years of living with a focus on my male energy, it's easy for me to slip back into my assertive male side. So I realize that I need a pretty masculine guy. Someone who enjoys being a man, as crazy as that may sound. I want a relationship with a guy who feels confident making decisions so that I don't feel drawn to jump in and take over."

Maggie glanced out at the trees and grinned. "I agree with you, but in defense of the men out there, I have to say that if I were dating you, I think that I'd defer many decisions to someone who seems to have an 'inside connection' with the spirit world. We all want an advantage in life, some 'insider information' that can make life easier. I mean, if you were a regular person and you were dating a guy with your abilities, wouldn't you be tempted to ask him to make most of the decisions?"

I frowned. "Well, yes..."

She smiled reassuringly. "I'm not saying that you can't share your gifts with a guy. I'm sure that it just requires some discipline on your end to not jump in and overrule decisions that he makes because you get a 'bad feeling' about it."

"True," I agreed, "but having both strong intuition and an enthusiastic personality means that keeping quiet about what I perceive is like roping a wild horse! Sometimes it's hard to find the balance between happily sharing how I see the world and intimidating the guy that I'm dating. But

I'm working on it."

Maggie smiled encouragingly. "And now that you've made me more aware of it, I'm going to pay attention to how much male energy I'm using when I'm on a date. I think that if I'm afraid the guy isn't taking me seriously, or if I'm feeling vulnerable in any way, then I tend to march out that strong male energy to take charge, and then I push him away. And then I wonder why he's pulled back! I'm glad that we talked about this. And I'm glad you shared that funny date story. This was a successful workout in so many ways!"

We parted ways and went off to work, both of us determined to pay more attention to when we were using our male energy and when we were using our female energy.

Chapter 11

―⊸◦〰◦⊱―

Susan's Follow-Up Session – If
I'm Perfect Am I Safe?

It had been two weeks since Susan had come for her first session, and today she was back in my treatment room looking frustrated and confused. This was causing her energy field to appear gray and scratchy, but the energy in her physical body actually looked a bit clearer, and she felt physically stronger to me. I don't see a lot of details when I look at someone's spirit—it appears to me like a white, filmy outline of the person—but I could feel Susan's spirit smiling and was curious to hear from Her but knew that I needed to let Susan vent her frustrations first.

"Well, I read all of the books that you suggested because I wanted to be the A student—that's my style," Susan began. "But I have to admit that I feel pretty disappointed. Several of the books talked about manifesting what you desire by changing your thoughts. I've been thinking about perfect health for over a week, but I still feel like I need all of the supplements that I brought in here last time!"

I reminded Susan that there was no rush to throw away her supplements.

"Yeah, but I understood from our last session that as I got better, I would know that I didn't need most of them anymore, so that's my barometer of how well I'm doing."

At this point, Susan's spirit held up Her hand as if to say, "Stop her there," so I asked Susan if she could pause and let me connect to her spirit. She looked ready to launch into a more thorough explanation of how the material in the books had not worked, but she closed her mouth and nodded her consent.

Susan's spirit came through sounding very gentle but firm. *"Susan puts tremendous pressure on herself to accomplish every task at lightning speed."*

"Yes, I'm very intense and enthusiastic about things," said Susan, smiling in agreement.

"Sometimes intensity is due to enthusiasm," responded Susan's spirit, *"and sometimes intensity is caused by fear. Susan's intensity is usually driven by fear, which blocks her natural intuition and leaves her processing everything with logic alone."*

"Fear of what?" Susan asked.

"The fear that things will not be alright until you accomplish whatever task is in front of you. That 'getting it all done right' is necessary in order for you to stay safe."

"Safe from what?!" As Susan's confusion increased, so did her level of frustration.

"When you were a small child, your mother had a very volatile temper."

"Well...yes, but what does that have to do with—"

"If you did not accurately gauge her desires and do things the way that she wanted them done, then trouble would ensue, right?"

"Yes, definitely. My sister and I would complain that Mom expected us to read her mind, but I got the worst of it because I was the oldest and Mom left me in charge. So if I didn't make the right things for dinner or make sure that my sister did her all of her homework, then there was trouble—lots of yelling, and sometimes I got hit."

"Just as hurtful as the physical punishments was the verbal abuse that you received. Your mother had very poor emotional containment, and so when she felt unpleasant emotions, she felt free to dump them all over you as a way of relieving some of the negative pressure that she was feeling inside.

"Because these verbal tirades were extremely upsetting and hurtful to you, you naturally sought to prevent them from reoccurring. You did this by trying to 'get it all right,' trying to anticipate what your mother wanted and what would keep her from getting angry. In this way, you sought to keep yourself safe—physically and emotionally."

I opened my eyes and looked at Susan. She was silently crying and dabbing at her eyes with a tissue. I focused on sending her loving, supportive energy, and she seemed to feel it because she looked directly at me and smiled.

"Please keep going—everything She's saying is right," Susan said.

"What you took from these childhood experiences is that when you get it wrong, very bad things can

happen to you, and no one will protect or help you. This idea formed in childhood, and you've been living by it ever since. It's the fear behind your urgency to get things right—at work and in every area of your life. And even though your mother has passed away, you've internalized her voice in your head. So when you determine that you could've done something in a better way, you play the tape in your head of your mother condemning you."

Susan looked surprised. "Oh my God, that *is* what I do! I know that people have told me that I'm hard on myself—my husband says that all the time—but I never realized that I'm talking to myself like my mother used to talk to me. Why would I do that?! Why would I continue to torture myself?"

"Because parents teach their children about the world, and so children assume that their parents' reactions are appropriate. Remember that when you were a toddler, your parents seemed to know the answer to everything—they're the ones that explained life to you. And as you matured, you realized on a conscious level that your mother's behavior was inappropriate and hurtful, but subconsciously it remained the norm for you. When you got things wrong, you still expected that type of condemning response—from someone. And when your mother wasn't around to provide it, you provided it for yourself as a way of policing your behavior.

"The first step in this process is to become aware of this pattern so that you can watch for it. Then when you notice you are talking to yourself harshly, imagine yourself as a child, and imagine speaking to a child instead of your adult self. Speak with

compassion and understanding, and see how much softer you can be with yourself. Try to imagine what the ideal response would be towards a child in that moment, and see if you can speak to yourself in that way."

"Wow. That's not what I thought this session would be about," Susan said thoughtfully.

I explained that a client's spirit has a thorough understanding of her entire spiritual journey and brings up each issue to cover at the time when the client is ready to heal it. Everything that's offered by a client's spirit is relevant to the healing journey, and I've learned to trust the order in which we cover things.

"Now, as to your complaints about the material presented in the books you've read," began Susan's spirit.

"Oh yes, that! I read the material about manifesting whatever you desire by understanding how thoughts create. And I've tried thinking about being perfectly healthy, but I don't see any evidence that it's working."

Susan's spirit responded, *"This frustration is a common occurrence when people begin learning about how thoughts create. But there are many thoughts generated by your mind each day, and it's quite a task to learn to direct a significant portion of them. Most people are only aware of a small percentage of their thoughts. For instance, how much time do you think that you spend—on an average day—thinking about your health?"*

Susan thought for a moment and then said, "About an hour a day."

"I would estimate that you spend nearly seven hours a day thinking about your health. You worry about how the food you eat is affecting you. You think about how much sleep you were able to get the night before, and how that will affect your body's functioning throughout the day. You monitor your body's symptoms for signs of negative change. And you question the supplements that you take with each meal and in between meals, wondering if they are beneficial to you. If you hear or read the words 'wellness, health, surgery, cancer, healing, or recovery,' you immediately think about your own health status.

"There are many triggers throughout each day, each one directing your thoughts back to your health. Each train of thought may last only thirty seconds, or you may dwell on it for several minutes, but throughout each day, you're not noticing how many of these negative thought tangents you're having.

"Now, how much time did you spend each day thinking positive, creative thoughts about your health and healing?"

Susan looked beaten. "About twenty minutes total. I did a ten-minute visualization each day and then tried to think good thoughts for a moment before each meal. So what's the solution? Quit my job so that I can spend all day focusing on happy thoughts about my health?"

"No, that's not necessary," responded her spirit patiently. *"It's important to recognize that if you're heavily invested in creating something, then there's a strong chance that you produce fearful thoughts on this subject throughout each day. Therefore it will*

be difficult to counterbalance each of those fearful thoughts to create what you desire.

"It's far easier to create something when you have less attachment to it, and therefore less fear about not achieving it. Start with simple things—a parking space close to the grocery store, or finding shrubbery for your yard that's on sale. Begin with creating items that you can request from the Universe without immediately producing fearful thoughts afterwards.

"If you try to create something over which you have no strong desire, then you're able to send the creative thought out into the Universe like you're ordering something at a restaurant. Once you place your order in a restaurant, you do not fret about whether or not the items you ordered will be brought to your table, you trust that they will arrive.

"Because you have so much fear that you will not regain great health, you're encouraged to begin by creating items of less importance. Once you see that this process works, you'll gain confidence in this method, and then you'll be able to release a request out into the Universe and trust that it is headed your way."

Susan looked concerned. "Does this ever fail to work? Do thoughts always produce the results that you want?"

"Everything in the physical world is relative, meaning that there are no absolutes here. So, in your wording, yes, there are times it doesn't work. There are several possible reasons why you may not produce something even when the majority of your thoughts about it are positive.

"The first is that it may not be in your best interest

to attain or experience that which you're asking for. Just because your ego desires something, that doesn't mean it's a good idea for you to have it. So you may send out positive thoughts creating that you get a job you interviewed for, but you may not get hired because there's a better job that will be available soon.

"When intense experiences happen to a person's body—a car accident or a serious illness like cancer— this does not mean that a person was not producing enough positive thoughts regarding such occurrences. It means that the person's spirit created the situation in order to accomplish specific goals. In your case the diagnosis of cancer thrust you on a journey of healing, both emotionally and physically. Prior to your cancer you rarely stopped to reflect on your stress levels and how things in your life affected you. Now you are more self-honoring, and you pay attention to how things feel intuitively. Cancer is never something that you would have chosen, but it has helped you accomplish tremendous personal growth."

"That makes sense. But I have to say that if I didn't get the job, or if I experience a recurrence of cancer or have a serious car accident, I will probably still feel depressed and frustrated even if I think my spirit wants me to experience such a thing."

"Yes, that's understandable. In fact, one way to understand and practice the concept of 'grace' is this: Think positive thoughts to create what you desire, and then accept what comes your way, regardless. Your job is to choose what you'd like to experience, request it clearly from the Universe, and then trust that what shows up for you is in your highest good.

This is not always easy to do."

"No kidding!" Susan laughed. "I'm sure I could be a great sport if I knew everything that my spirit knows. But from my limited perspective down here, it just looks like these rules that I'm learning about the Universe don't really work. Then I start to feel foolish, like I believed something because I wanted it to be true, not because it logically made sense."

"Yes, and then you constrict with negative emotions, pulling your energy back and wrapping it tightly around yourself, shutting out your connection with Me. This is also called 'losing faith'."

Susan nodded her head vigorously. "Yes, I've certainly had that experience!"

"Regaining great health is in your best interest, and the Universe supports this desire of yours. But the journey will involve numerous steps, and this process will give you the opportunity to heal many of your inaccurate beliefs as well as your physical body. It also will allow you to meet valuable friends, teachers, and healers. So do not judge the effectiveness of your creating or of your healing process simply by the speed at which your body heals. There is healing happening on many levels, and there is more than one agenda being served. And some of these agendas are beyond the scope of your current understanding."

Susan took a moment to let that message sink in. "Okay, so how should I move forward?"

"Your role is to choose what you want—in this case thorough healing of your body and your beliefs about health—and to monitor your thoughts to ensure that you're staying positive on this subject. You'll

also need to sit quietly for some period of time each day in order to feel guidance from Me. I will send you guidance—in the form of feelings and ideas—to help you accomplish your goal. So you may feel guided to contact a new doctor that you've heard about or be drawn to buy a book that you saw in the store. In this way, I will help you move forward."

We finished Susan's session with an energy treatment and my offer to confirm messages for her that she felt came from her spirit.

Follow-up:

Susan is learning to trust her body, although she would assert that this is much easier to do when her body is feeling healthy and strong! She has not had a bladder infection or a sinus infection for nearly a year but will notice her symptoms begin to return when she falls back into old (fearful) beliefs about her body and her health.

Susan has been working with her spirit to recognize some of the effects of her difficult childhood, and as she extends compassion towards herself and her memories, she has healed emotionally. As her emotionally healing has progressed, her drive towards perfectionism has lessened, and her creativity and productivity have increased dramatically.

Susan is working on using her thoughts to intentionally create the life she chooses and is enjoying the resulting feeling of empowerment.

Chapter 12

Justin Runs for Class President

When people ask me if my boys are much different than other kids their age, my first impulse is to assert that they are typical teenagers, leaving socks all over the house and playing more video games than I would prefer. Then some small event occurs, and I realize how different their perspective is compared to the average person's viewpoint. Today a client asked me what I say to my boys when they ask why the world isn't fair, and it made me remember Justin's brief run at politics.

Years ago when Justin was in the fifth grade, he came home one day and announced that he'd decided to run for class president. The election was the next day, and this was the first time I'd heard him mention any interest in school politics, let alone running for the top seat. Knowing that such elections are frequently just popularity contests, I asked Justin some questions to discover if he had any real interest in helping to govern his class. Nope, he didn't seem to have any such altruistic aspirations. He seemed primarily interested in the popularity aspect of the elections and the feeling of power he might attain if he was allowed to influence some classroom policies.

Since the election was the next afternoon, Justin went upstairs to write the speech that he would deliver the following morning. Now I'm a proud mother who believes in her son's brilliance, but even I know that any election speech written in twenty minutes probably won't be awe-inspiring. So as Justin read me his hastily prepared speech, I had to choose my words carefully. I suggested that he may want to do more than just tell jokes and offered one or two suggestions. He brushed aside my ideas and remained confident in his approach. "Nah, it's fine Mom. The kids in my grade already know who I am anyway." I let it go, thinking that it might end up being a lesson in humility and in choosing public service.

The next day Justin came home from school very indignant. He had not won the position of class president (no surprise to me) and was annoyed at the class choice, a girl who was not particularly popular. Justin was resentful and seemed to feel entitled to an explanation.

"Mom, this doesn't seem fair! I know that more kids like me than Becky, and she's so shy, I don't even know if she will ask the school office to make any changes! Can you go ask my spirit right now why I didn't win?"

I knew better than to try and give him a meaningful answer while he was so annoyed, instead I made a bargain with him. "Justin, I'll sit down and ask my spirit, if you go up to your room, connect to your spirit, and ask the same question. Okay?"

He grumbled about this requirement because of course the easiest thing to do is to sit on the sofa and let me raise my energy up and retrieve the answers for him. But while I was a long way from getting my boys to sit and meditate every day, I was still able to convince them to connect to their spirits when they needed to get answers. So he trudged up the stairs and shut his door.

About fifteen minutes later, he appeared before me with tears in his eyes. "Mom, I get it now, it's all fine," he said and then started to walk away.

"Wait a minute, wait a minute," I said as I followed him into the kitchen. "What did your spirit say to you?"

"He said that the election results were fair because what needed to happen is just what happened. He said that last year Becky ran for class president and didn't win. And this year her parents are getting a divorce, and she feels kind of like no one really sees her or hears her right now, and so she really needs to be president. Mom, if I'd known that, I wouldn't have even run against her! I'm glad that she won—I want her to be class president. I think that it *is* fair."

I had to blink back tears; I was moved by his true empathy. That's when it felt right to convey to him what my spirit had told me years earlier about the subject of fairness.

"Justin, my understanding of this world is that it is *completely* fair. The reason why we frequently don't see it that way is because we look at things through our ego's desires. Our ego wants to have everything feel fair in this instant, which means according to the way that our ego thinks fair should look. My spirit has explained to me that the Universe is very fair, but the Universe's definition of fairness is not based on our ego's opinions.

"The Universe defines fairness to mean that every person gets to experience exactly what his spirit chooses for him to experience. Each of us is taken care of—our spirit makes sure of that—and we each receive what we need, for our growth and for our best experience. And sometimes what we need is contrast, like you received today. Sometimes when things feel bad, we stop and look around, trying to figure things out. And then we have realizations, understandings, growth. So even though our ego isn't pleased, we *are* always getting what we need to help us take the next step."

Justin grasped the concept immediately and went upstairs to do his homework. As I went back to my desk, I wondered how differently my life would have been if I had known this definition of fairness as a child. We were all raised with the saying, "Life isn't fair, get used to it." This left me feeling vulnerable and anxious because there were apparently no rules to the game, no referee keeping things predictable or safe. Now I feel less anxious and fearful, knowing that whatever happens, I am being looked after. I may not enjoy what happens in my daily life, but I can rest assured that it is happening for a reason, not just because "Sh** just happens" (another adage I'd love to erase from our culture).

This knowledge has made such a profound difference in my life, so I try to convey the concept to my clients and kids so that they can live with less fear also. Once we understand that things are happening "*for* us" not "*to* us," our reactions change. This doesn't mean that I never get resentful or fearful—I definitely do! But within a short period of time, I remember that I've been given *so* much evidence of how the Universe is always conspiring to help each of us. So either I can focus on the evidence in front of me that my ego believes is proof that no one is helping me and that I'm all alone in my struggles, or I can look for evidence of how I am being encouraged to shift in some way—to grow, to learn, to achieve better balance.

Of course, I had to chuckle a few weeks later when Justin delivered my teachings right back to me. I was in search of a particular type of avocado tree to take to my father for Father's Day. I called different nurseries and found one that had them in stock. I loaded the boys in the car and headed off for the nursery. Thirty minutes later we arrived to find the nursery closed and the gates locked. UGH!! I was so frustrated. How could they be closed?! They were open just thirty minutes ago, they knew I was coming, and it was the middle of a Saturday! I sat fuming in the car, refusing to drive away and "give up."

The boys listened to me rant for a moment, quietly sitting in the back seat, probably recoiling from the negative energy I was spewing. Then Justin's voice piped up and innocently asked, "Mom, you said that everything happens for a reason, and that the Universe is always trying to help us. So why don't you just ask your spirit why this happened, and then you won't have to be mad anymore?"

I wanted to snap at him, "Because I'm so mad that I can't get my energy high enough to ask Her anything right now!" But luckily I took a deep breath instead. I think I mumbled something about wanting to get home, and that I would sit and meditate then, and I turned the car around and headed home. But after a few minutes of driving, I had to laugh and allow myself to feel grateful that my son had absorbed such an important lesson that his first reaction to an unpleasant event was to assume a valid, helpful reason was behind it. And then I had to deal with my feelings of embarrassment because my son was acting more evolved and enlightened than I was.

When I got back home I called my brother to ask him if he wanted to join together to get a Father's Day gift. He said "Oh, I'm glad that you called! I drove by a nursery this morning and saw big avocado trees on sale, so I went ahead and picked one up for us to give to Dad. I remembered you saying that he wanted one, and these were really beautiful and on sale! So don't buy one, we're already set with the gift." I had mixed emotions as I found my boys and told them about the tree that their uncle had already purchased. I was impressed by the Universe, and a little embarrassed that I had to be reminded—yet again!—that the Universe is always conspiring on our behalf.

Chapter 13

Alan's Case – Having a Voice, Being Included

Alan was my next client. He was referred to me by his gastroenterologist who had sheepishly handed him my business card and said, "I don't really know how to explain what she does, but she seems to help people with gastro issues who don't want to take medications."

Alan owns several very successful BMW car dealerships throughout southern California. He's been married for almost twenty-seven years to his wife, Debbie, and they have four children: two in college and two in high school. When Alan came in for this first session, he assumed that the focus would be on his business, as it operates at a very intense pace and therefore was assumed to be the culprit in his bouts with irritable bowel syndrome. So he was surprised when his spirit's questions focused on his relationships at home.

"Would you say that you feel empowered at work?" Alan's spirit asked. When Alan's facial expression told me that he didn't understand the question, I

offered some help.

"I think your spirit is asking if you feel like you are seen and heard and respected at your company."

"Oh! Sure, absolutely," Alan said confidently.

"And at home?" his spirit asked.

"Uh, I guess so," Alan offered with considerably less confidence than his previous answer.

"Who would you say your children have more respect for—you or your wife?"

"Oh, Julia for sure!" said Alan. "She's the one that makes the rules and runs the show at home. I mean, we both make the rules for the kids, but she enforces them on a daily basis."

His spirit continued, *"Do you feel that you have a strong voice in your family? By that I mean that if you make a request or express a concern or preference, is it recognized as being of equal weight to that of Julia's preferences and concerns?"*

Alan thought for a moment. "My first instinct is to say yes, but ya' know...the answer is probably no. I'm not saying that she's a bully," Alan said in a rush, "'cause she's not. But she likes things done her way. And I guess I've learned to just let her run things her way when it comes to the house and kids."

I could feel his spirit leaning in, which meant that He wanted Alan to continue. "Can you say more about how you 'learned to just let her run those things'?" I asked.

Alan looked uncomfortable. He reminded me of someone who didn't want to get in trouble for tattling on a friend. "Well, Julia's great—she's a great mom and wife," he began diplomatically, "but she can be a bit...tough. In the past, when she felt like I disagreed with her decisions at home, she got very defensive and upset. So most of the time, I just decide that it isn't worth bringing it up. We agree on most things, and the differences are on pretty small items."

I had a feeling that those "small items" were adding up for Alan.

Alan's spirit chimed in, *"And she has also made it clear that you have your business and she has hers, which is the running of the family."*

"Yes! I know that she feels that way. One time when I questioned how many after-school activities she had to drive the kids to, she told me that she doesn't come down to the dealerships to tell me how to run my business, so I should let her do her job without criticism. And since, overall, she does a fantastic job, I decided to butt out."

"Can you agree that there is a difference between one of your managers offering a suggestion to you versus telling you that he could run your business better than you can?"

Alan smiled. "Sure. The first action I see as valuable. The second one might get you fired."

"As a child, your wife rarely received praise from her father. If he commented on her or her behavior, it was usually in the form of harsh criticisms."

I opened my eyes and saw that Alan was nodding his head vigorously in agreement, so I continued.

"Because of this, your wife is sensitive to potential criticism, especially from the men in her life. So she has perceived your comments and preferences to be questions of how she performs her job. In order to

protect herself from feeling criticized, she has tried to block you from offering any feedback. But this relegates you to having a very small voice within your family."

Alan looked intrigued. "So how exactly has she blocked me from having a voice? By getting upset when I offer suggestions and feedback?"

"It seems to be a two-step process. First she has a negative emotional reaction—getting defensive, crying, or yelling—which makes you feel uncomfortable. Then she pulls away from you, which leaves you feeling abandoned emotionally."

"Yeah! I call it 'being left out in the cold.' Like the dog she forgot to bring in from the snowy backyard."

"One way to condition someone's behavior is to disconnect from him energetically. Because we are all dependent on being energetically connected to those around us, when we feel completely cut-off from someone else's energy, it sets off alarm bells within us that something is very wrong. Because we want to reestablish that connection, we try to avoid repeating the behavior that resulted in being cut off. Shutting someone out energetically can be a very powerful way of conditioning his behavior."

"I'll say!" agreed Alan.

"Out of the loyalty and love you feel for your wife, you agreed with her presumption that your suggestions were criticisms."

"What? No, wait a minute—I don't think that! I disagree!" contested Alan.

"Your actions indicate otherwise to Julia. By discontinuing your attempts to be a part of the decision-making process at home, you validated her

fears that your motivation was to be critical. I suggest that when you voice an opinion or suggestion, be clear that it is not meant as a criticism, just participation in the family decisions. Would you allow your managers to assert that any suggestions you make are the equivalent of criticizing their work?"

Alan scoffed. "No, that would be ridiculous. Receiving constructive criticism is part of being an adult with a job— Oh, I see your point!"

"Julia is sensitive to hearing constructive criticism because she hears it as primarily disapproval and judgment. But since you do not intend to berate her, you must advocate for yourself and for your place in the conversation. You will need to be careful as you monitor your tone of voice and take care not to sound impatient or judgmental, but having no voice is not working for you.

"It does not serve anyone to play small in order to keep the peace. And having to feel powerless in your own home in order to keep a loving connection to your wife is simply an unhealthy price to pay. And it is not necessary. It is far better to clear up the inaccurate assumptions that she has regarding your intentions than to keep quiet once you walk in your front door."

"I get it, but how does this relate to my IBS symptoms?" Alan asked.

"It is a difficult shift that you make each day, from being in charge and feeling very respected, to coming home and feeling rather shut down. You've rationalized not being able to say much regarding the choices your wife and kids make by thinking that you're very tired from making decisions all day

at work. But the truth is that it is quite difficult to transition from feeling very seen and heard and respected, to feeling almost invisible at times."

"Yeah, my spirit is right. I do always say that I'm fine with not voicing an opinion because I feel like people are after me all day to make decisions. But I guess I would like to feel included in what's happening at home too. I'm not saying that Julia is awful—I feel like we're beating up on her in here."

"The goal of this session is not to make anyone 'wrong.' It is to help you see how an unhealthy aspect of an otherwise loving marriage is causing your body to be symptomatic. Those physical symptoms are there to alert you to an imbalance in your life. Imbalances like this one arise when one or both people in a relationship have a wound that is clouding how things are understood. My goal is to help you understand that by walking around Julia's wound about receiving feedback, you have agreed to adjust your relationship so that she is not uncomfortable. But sometimes feeling discomfort can be beneficial as it prompts you to look at unhealed wounds that are affecting how you perceive the world around you.

"By agreeing to have a tiny voice in your family matters, you essentially hand over most of your power when you get home. This feeling of powerlessness— that you're hesitant to speak for fear of unpleasant repercussions—causes negative energy to be present in the bowel area. This is an area of the body where we vibrate when we are feeling powerful, or in this case, a lack of power. Having a lot of negative energy here greatly compromises the bowel functioning."

"So helping Julia get comfortable with me adding

my two cents in to family stuff, this will help me feel more powerful at home, which will make this area of my body healthier?"

"In a word, yes. Your symptoms are the result of feeling that you have to hand over your power in order to keep the peace. This rarely happens at your car dealerships but happens with regularity at home. You intuitively know that the current way of living isn't quite right, but you're unsure of how to adjust it, so you've continued this way for some time. Your body's symptoms are motivating you to keep pushing for a better resolution, like the approach that we've discussed today."

"Wow! I've gotta say, I'm surprised. I mean, you're right—my spirit is right, I just didn't think that my wife and I, that our relationship, would be the problem. My business is so intense, and people who watch me running all five dealerships comment on how amazed they are that I can handle that much stress. So I just assumed that I would come in here, and you would tell me that I had to cut back my hours or something."

"Your business is very successful and the pace is rather intense, as you said, but you have done a good job of hiring skillful people to work for you, and you are adept at delegating work to them. So while your day is very busy, it does not typically create feelings of being overwhelmed and disempowered. Having a bit more time to relax each day would be healthful for you, but this is advice that applies to most people in your culture."

"Agreed!" laughed Alan. "Okay, I'm going to talk to Julia and convince her that I'm lovingly participating, not critically analyzing!"

I was pleased to see Alan's energy field look much stronger than when he arrived. I gave him an energy treatment, focusing lots of healing energy in his lower abdomen, and sent him on his way.

Follow-up:

Two weeks later Alan sent me an email to update me on his symptoms. He said that his conversation with Julia seemed to go well, but that she had continued to protest his questions and comments about the daily family activities. He reported that he was undaunted because he did not want to go back to validating her beliefs since they were not accurate. So he continued to participate in the family dynamics and showered his wife with loving affection at the same time. "She couldn't help but enjoy my participation then!" Alan wrote, and I could picture him laughing and grinning as he wrote it.

Three months later I saw Alan and his wife Julia for a couple's session. They could feel themselves slipping back into their old pattern and wanted their spirits' help to continue moving forward. Julia's spirit helped her recognize particular subjects and words that triggered the resurfacing of old wounds from her childhood, and Alan's spirit helped him choose more neutral words that he could use instead. They now have a list of "loving words"—phrases that have a pre-defined meaning between them and that are to be used to support and reassure rather than critique.

Alan's IBS symptoms have diminished to such

a degree that his doctors have declared him "in remission," and Alan talks to his customers and employees about his healing journey and its resulting benefits to all of his relationships.

Chapter 14

Imprisoned by My Categories

I was working with a client today and her spirit talked to her about how we often create our own suffering by thinking in terms of absolute categories. I wanted to offer some of that information here, but don't want to reveal her story because she's an actress and has plenty of privacy issues already. So I'll share a lesson I learned about my own categories a few years ago.

I was at lunch with a friend, and as I talked to her, I realized that the six years after my divorce were the first time that I had truly experienced severe, ongoing financial stress. Which is strange because I'd experienced being the "starving student" waiting for the student-loan check to arrive, and the law student with school loans in the six-figure range. But those six years were the only time in my life that I can remember lying awake at night worrying about what would happen if I didn't make more money. Until now. I could sound logical and assert that this increased level of fear was reasonable and rational since I had two boys to support and a hefty mortgage, etc. But while that is true, I have to admit to a different reason for feeling all that fear—it was the first time that I had seen myself as part of the struggling masses.

During lunch my friend said that she stopped being so nervous about money when someone explained to her that money is just congealed energy, and that it flows into and out of your experience. Remember that, she advised, and it will demystify the whole concept of money as this rare thing that you have to hunt down.

The problem was that I already knew that—I've taught my students this concept for years. And as I opened my mouth to pronounce this to her, recounting how I used to give lectures on the subject of money, I realized with a sinking heart that I'd held that belief once before, but had somehow lost it. By lost I don't mean that I forgot that belief, just that I didn't seem to be able to believe it anymore. My brain immediately screamed, "Why not?" and within seconds, I had my answer—because I no longer felt special.

I was raised by parents who seemed to know that they were special. They would deny this fact of course, as they are both quite humble, but inside I believe that they were always aware that they were the exception to the rule—to many rules. They got married as teenagers and are still happily married fifty years later, which in itself is exceptional. They got pregnant right away with me (I've always been rather impatient to get out in the world), and so neither of them went off to attend a four-year college, even though they're both very intelligent. My father started a company, and together they run a corporation that's considered one of the top in its field. It was always a dream for both of them to adopt children from other countries, so in addition to my two birth brothers, I have four siblings who are adopted from Korea.

I remember living in some very modest apartments when I was young, but now my parents live in a big beautiful house in Malibu. Our family is loud, liberal, biracial, and filled with bright, funny people. And just as our family is quite different than the average family, I grew up thinking of myself as different.

I was a good student in school and was aware that I was smart and enjoyed learning. When my brother and I were sent to Catholic Bible Study classes on Wednesday afternoons (my father's parents were very Catholic and strongly recommended we attend these), I got in trouble for asking questions of the nuns. I saw it as perfectly reasonable to question where the animals on Noah's ark went to the bathroom and how they kept the tigers from eating the gazelles. My questions were met with frowns and reprimands, and at times I was sent out to sit in the hall. I was relieved when my mother gave me permission to question everyone and everything. "If it can't stand up to questioning, then it's not something worth believing in," she'd say. With that statement, my mother gave me permission to think for myself and to operate outside of the rules "if I had a good reason."

This theme of "the rules don't always apply to you" also came up with my aunt Sandy, a very smart (and admittedly bossy) woman who was an influential part of my childhood. One day we were in the car, and as she ignored a traffic sign at the entrance to a freeway, she declared, "Some rules are here just for the people who can't quickly figure out the right thing to do." I understood her as saying that if you're smart, you have permission to make your own rules. Since I was getting good grades in school and impressing my teachers, I guess I concluded that I was in this "special" category, and because of this fact, I didn't expect to have a typical life experience.

Not that I thought I would be famous—I have never desired that sort of life—but I didn't want or expect to struggle with things that the average person struggled with. And guess what? I didn't! And when I did get sick or found myself short on money, I believed that the episode would be short-lived, and so it always was. And since thoughts create, I seemed to glide through life with relative ease. In other words, nothing rocked my perspective, my belief that I was living outside of the normal life experience.

Until my divorce.

No one in my immediate family had ever gotten a divorce, and the subject wasn't really discussed. My parents occasionally argued, but there was never a moment where I worried that they would separate. They are lifelong partners, and they taught us kids to see marriage as a special union that gave you strength and made life more enjoyable. They're not strictly religious, so we never felt pressured into respecting marriage out of moral or religious obligations. Divorce was just something that didn't seem to happen in our family—we were that large, funny family that most of my friends envied. My parents were considered cool when I was a teenager, and my friends used to prefer hanging out at my house over their own. In a word, my family seemed "charmed," undaunted by the obstacles in life that hobble other "regular" families. We had a few difficulties, but to the outsider we always seemed to sail a bit above the clouds.

Without me even realizing it, divorce had made me feel like I'd been tossed into some sort of "discard pile," like the cards that have been put down on the table when you're playing blackjack. I was still part of the deck, just the disposable part. And it wasn't just the divorce itself, it was the events that followed. It was the teacher who told me that she wasn't surprised that my son was having trouble in her class since he "came from a divorced family." And it was hearing the phrase I came to loathe: "failed marriage." (When friendships end, we say that we grew apart. Why are marriages listed as failed when they end?) Or the pity that people sent my way when I told them I was in the middle of a divorce. Those people meant well, but their sympathy-filled looks made me feel that I must be worthy of pity. If you're worthy of pity, then you must not be leading a charmed life, right? So over the months, I received these messages, which matched my miserable experience of divorce, and when it was over, I had been kicked out of the "charmed life" category. And I didn't even realize it for almost six years. Damn! I'd spent over five years struggling to get back on my feet financially, and I hadn't even realized that I'd landed in a category that made escaping financial struggles nearly impossible.

So the critical question was: How can I get back in the category where I'm living a charmed life? I didn't have the answer to that question, so I sat down to connect to my spirit and ask for Her advice.

Journal entry
conversation with Spirit
March 10, 2010

Spirit, I realize that I used to see myself as living outside of the normal financial struggles that burden most people, and because of this perception, I lived with less financial struggle than nearly everyone I knew. But since my divorce, I have lumped myself into the same category as everyone else, and just as before, my thoughts are playing a huge role in creating my experience. What do You suggest?

My spirit: *"You're correct that your beliefs and thoughts control much of your experience with money. When you believed that you were not limited to the same financial struggles that most people lived with, money flowed to you in extraordinary ways. Do you remember how the Universe presented you with incredible savings, extra income from a variety of sources, and the experience of prosperity even when your husband's business was struggling? You didn't believe that your experience would be like everyone else's, and so you looked for the differences between their lives and yours.*

"There are always differences—and there are always similarities—between you and the people around you. There are times where it will benefit you to focus on the similarities, like when you want to deepen your compassion. Everyone suffers, and when we can identify with someone else's suffering, it's natural to extend compassion and forgiveness.

"But if you don't want to have an experience that's common to the average person, such as financial strife, then you're advised to focus on the differences between yourself and those around you. In the past, you perceived yourself as intelligent, resourceful, and skillful in business matters. You credited your family with helping you acquire these skills, but the skill set belonged to you. Do you still possess these skills?"

Yes. But my life seems to be less charmed and more... ordinary. And so I guess I changed the expectations of what I thought my life would look like.

My Spirit: "Yes, you did. But you can change your expectations yet again, and your life will change accordingly. It's the essential character of a person, not just her life circumstances, that determines the 'category' that she lives in. There are many people who come from 'ordinary' circumstances but lead extraordinary lives. This is partially because the person's spirit has chosen this path of experiences before incarnating, and partially because the individual sees herself as different and holds different expectations for herself. She does not limit her life experiences to what she sees others going through, *but uses such observations as a starting point.*

"Think of it like a menu. The waitress tells you that most people in that restaurant order the chicken dish. Would you assume that the chicken dish is what you would enjoy the most?"

No, because I know that my favorite foods might not be everyone else's, so I would read the whole menu and then decide.

My Spirit: *"Exactly! You would consider what others are experiencing (and choosing), and then you would decide what felt good for you after looking at all the possibilities. What the people around you are having is one option. If it looks unappealing, find a reason why you can have a different experience. There will always be plenty of ways to distinguish yourself from others and plenty of reasons to convince yourself that you're going to have similar struggles.*

"If you don't like the experiences that you're having in an area of your life, determine which category you've placed yourself in and see if it serves you. Frequently the 'average person' category will be unsatisfactory to you since most people believe that life is hard, and so they create a lot of resistance for themselves. But it's always up to you to decide which category you want to be in."

I understand what You're saying. I've met people who perceived themselves as beautiful or highly intelligent, and the general public probably would not have agreed with their assessments of themselves. But they were leading lives as if they were these things, and I could see that this was because their belief was so strong that they drew those experiences towards themselves.

Alright, I'm going to work my way back to seeing myself as different from the "average person," so that I can expect my life to show up without all the financial drama that most people endure. Thanks!

End of journal entry

I'm happy to report that as I looked for the differences between myself and the average person, I found them. I used these as rationalizations for why I might have different financial experiences, and my financial issues began to disappear! I'm not fabulously wealthy yet (still working on that), but I no longer have sleepless nights worrying about money. I know that the first step in ending my extreme financial stress was recognizing and changing the category I had placed myself into.

Often when my clients feel that they've worked hard to change an aspect of their life and not made much progress, their spirits help them see how they've placed themselves into a category that limits the success that they can experience. To unveil some of the categories that may be limiting your success, write down a topic that you would like to change in your life. Then quickly and honestly list off all the things that will have to happen before that change can occur. Now on a separate piece of paper, think of people different than yourself—people who already have this success that you want to create for yourself. List what they have to do to create or maintain this success. Put the list aside for a few minutes and breathe deeply to re-center yourself. Compare the two lists, and see if you can label or describe the two categories. How can you step from the category that you're in now over to the other category where it's easier to create what you desire? What do you already have in common with the people in that category? This exercise can raise your awareness and help you shift your life experience!

Chapter 15

―∘◦⟨⟨⟨∘⟩⟩⟩◦∘―

Kevin's Case – Honor and Self Advocacy

W hen the doorbell rang and I approached my front door, I could feel interesting energy on the other side. It was 11:30 a.m., so I knew that this energy belonged to my next appointment, a new client named Kevin. The energy felt very solid and contained. It felt like the energy of someone who had served in the military, and I half expected to open the door and find a uniformed man saluting me. As I opened the door, Kevin smiled, and I could feel the warmth of his personality as well as his strong energy.

Kevin was sent to me by his dentist, a very caring man who was baffled by Kevin's dental/medical history. Kevin has two different autoimmune conditions in his mouth, both of which are quite rare. Dr. Hinton, Kevin's dentist, had never seen a patient with both conditions, and he thought it was worth investigating the emotional issues that were contributing to the poor condition of Kevin's teeth and gums. My work is far outside of Kevin's comfort zone, but out of desperation, he agreed to come see me when Western medicine had run out of answers for him.

After Kevin gave me his dental history, I asked him about his life. He said that he was dating a woman that he felt very compatible with, and his energy glowed a nice shade of pink as he spoke of her, confirming that he was happy in that relationship. Kevin said that his work as a controller in a biomedical research firm was fairly stressful, but that he knew that he was good at his job. When I asked why the job was stressful, Kevin talked about his boss, a loud, egotistical man who blamed others when things went wrong. Because Kevin held a high position at the company, plenty of blame landed on him when his boss began ranting. Kevin didn't seem too angry about this, and when I inquired further, he commented, "Well, it's like my dad always said, 'If you can't handle the bad parts without whining, you don't deserve the good parts'."

"Tell me more about your dad," I encouraged.

"He's Russian, and a very strong, proud man. He wanted me to go into the military to learn discipline, and he was proud when I did well as a Marine. He was tough to grow up with—you never felt like what you did was good enough—but he was fair."

I wondered about that last comment, thinking that Kevin's father and I might define fairness a bit differently. I closed my eyes and connected to Kevin's spirit to get feedback on what Kevin had shared. His spirit told me that Kevin's father lived according to very black and white categories, and the rules around those categories were quite rigid.

His father believed that being a "team player" was essential to survival—both in the family and in the world—and if you were a team player, you agreed to never contradict the leader of the team. Kevin's spirit suggested that I ask Kevin what happened if he disagreed with his father.

"Well, usually we just kept quiet about it—me, my brother, and my mom. Sometimes Mom would quietly bring up something, and Dad might listen, but usually his response was to yell. He would say that no one appreciated how hard he worked to provide for all of us, and then he would storm off and not talk much for the next day or two. Mom would say, 'Well, your father's right, he does work awfully hard to take care of us.' And what she was telling us was to be alright with whatever Dad decided because that's how we could show that we were team players who appreciated him and all his efforts."

"So in order to be a good family member, you had to agree to be mute?" asked Kevin's spirit.

"Oh, no! We were allowed to speak. It just wasn't worth saying things that would upset Dad or Mom."

"So, to clarify, you were allowed to speak your truth as long as it didn't contradict your dad's truth or upset your mother."

"Well, when You say it like that it sounds kind of ridiculous," grumbled Kevin.

"It also sounds like your current work place," said Kevin's spirit. *"From an early age, you connected the idea of support with compliance. To contradict someone or to voice a differing opinion signified a lack of appreciation and respect. And the military training that you received reinforced this idea. So*

now if you were to set boundaries about how your boss speaks to you, it would feel like you were devaluing the company and its importance in your life. Since you're clear that your job is important to you, you accept whatever treatment is offered to you as a sign of respect."

"Yes, I guess I can see that," said Kevin thoughtfully.

"It's frequently critical in the military for everyone to work together as a team, and at times this means putting aside individual ideas and opinions in order to keep cohesion in the group. Lives often depend on a unit moving as one, and this means having a leader who is followed without question. But this is not true in every moment, and it's certainly not true in civilian life. Is it accurate to say that the men who advance to the highest levels in the military think independently and voice their opinions when they think it may benefit the group?"

"Yes, that's true," Kevin agreed.

"In fact you could say that it's often how the next generation of leaders is chosen—from those who distinguish themselves as willing to suggest something different than the status quo."

"Okay, I can go with that," Kevin nodded.

Kevin's spirit then asked, *"Do you believe that these men who question the status quo have lost respect for the military or for their country?"*

"No, not at all!" said Kevin. "I think that the true leaders want their unit to succeed, and that's why they're willing to stick their necks out to suggest changes that would benefit everyone. Oh, I see where You're going with this." Kevin seemed to slump a bit in his chair.

"You are a team player," Kevin's spirit continued, *"but sometimes being a truly valuable team player means not playing it safe. It means speaking up when things aren't handled fairly and holding people accountable—even the people who rank above you. The rigid rules that your father insisted that his family follow were not about creating a strong team. They were for the purpose of eliminating any challenges to his authority and control. That doesn't create a strong and healthy team, it creates a dictatorship.*

"Do you truly believe that your boss is always right, and that your ideas and opinions should be ignored?" asked Kevin's spirit.

"No," Kevin answered, "but I also don't think that a company would run very well if everyone was allowed to say whatever they wanted to in every moment. Then people would be mouthing off and starting disagreements, and nothing would ever get done."

"You're thinking in extremes, like the black and white categories that your dad used," said Kevin's spirit. *"There's a middle ground where people don't say everything that pops into their head, but they also don't withhold important feedback because it might cause discomfort. What is being suggested is that you release the automatic assumption that if you offer a different perspective that it will cause a weakening of your team and signal disrespect of the organization.*

"It may help you to write down your thoughts before you share them with your boss. This way you can review them and make sure that you're not just reacting in the moment. If you assess what you've

written down and find that it could be helpful to your performance and to your integrity as an employee, then you're encouraged to voice your thoughts.

"I understand that you have been raised to be respectful of authority and of the organization that you are a part of, but were you also raised to be respectful of yourself?"

"Yeah, definitely," Kevin responded quickly. "I was taught to take pride in my appearance and to take care of my body by working out and eating right."

"Yes, this is how you respect your physical body, but I'm wondering how you respect your emotional body."

"Umm...I don't really know what You mean," said Kevin.

"Have you noticed that, in comparison to some of your friends and lovers, you don't seem to experience a lot of highs and lows emotionally?"

"Yes, in fact previous girlfriends have complained that I'm too flat emotionally. They like it when I don't get worked up about things when we disagree, but I don't get very excited about things either. I just figured that this was my personality type."

"Your personality is quite calm, but it's not as flat as you're describing. That flatness is because you learned at an early age to suppress your emotions. Your father and mother made it clear that there was only room for your dad's large emotions, and so everyone else in the family had to contain and suppress theirs. Since everyone has feelings— not just your father—this was disrespectful to everyone else when only your father was allowed to express feelings."

"Wow. I never looked at it like that before," murmured Kevin.

"In your current job, only your boss is allowed to express his feelings, and he often does so in an abusive way. Respecting yourself emotionally means noticing when it feels like someone is disrespecting you and setting up boundaries to stop such behavior. This will usually not look like yelling back at him. It will consist of you gathering your thoughts by writing down how you're feeling and then talking calmly to your boss about a better way to handle such situations. When you are clear how you should be treated and why, then your energy will feel strong as you speak to him, and you are more likely be heard and respected."

"And what if I'm not?" Kevin asked.

"Then you will have to decide if you want to keep working for someone who does not respect you. This is not meant to worry you about having to leave your current job. I mean to help you learn to respect yourself as much as you respect others in positions of authority. When you have achieved this, then you will speak more freely and more wisely, and your mouth will no longer contain so much negative energy."

"Wait— What?" Kevin asked. "What's causing the negative energy there?"

"When your boss is frustrated and blowing off steam by yelling at you, you have a healthy reaction to his behavior—you feel frustrated. This is appropriate. Your discomfort tells you that something is 'off' in how you're being treated. But instead of saying anything, you suppress your feelings and hold your tongue. By squelching your verbal response,

you hold onto that negative energy and walk away chewing on the angry words that you didn't say out loud. Think of this negative energy sitting in your mouth and weakening the tissues in that area of your body."

"So in order to not have negative energy in my mouth, do I need to spit out those angry words and scream back at my boss?" Kevin asked.

"No, but those thoughts and feelings should be released somehow. Writing them down would be sufficient, particularly until you feel comfortable enough to voice your opinions. The idea here is that always keeping quiet is costing you. The price you pay is your health—emotionally and physically."

Kevin rubbed his temples. "Boy, this seems like an overhaul of my whole personality. I'm not used to speaking my mind."

"You won't be able to change this in one day, so don't expect that from yourself. And it's not a change to your entire personality. In your personal relationships, you frequently speak your truth. You don't regard such people as having authority over you, and so you feel more freedom to voice your opinions."

"Unless it gets heated. Then I clam up!" Kevin sounded exasperated with himself.

"That's understandable," his spirit offered soothingly. *"Growing up, there were not many times where things got slightly heated and then settled back down. Frequently when anyone got even a little emotional as they spoke, your father 'blew up,' and his big reaction overshadowed everyone else's feelings."*

"Yeah! It's like he was this fire that sucked all

the air out of the room so that there wasn't enough oxygen for anyone else to have even a small spark of a reaction," Kevin added.

"This behavior provided strong incentive for everyone to keep their emotions in check so as not to cause a big explosion from your father. And it has carried over into your adult life so that you're uncomfortable expressing strong emotions, fearing that they will quickly lead to an out-of-control situation."

Kevin looked contemplative and nodded his head in agreement.

"But now you can recognize where this behavior pattern stems from and realize that you're no longer living with someone who behaves in that way. You choose people in your personal life who have healthy boundaries when it comes to their emotional responses, and so I want you to feel free to begin expressing how you feel. This will quickly feel liberating, especially when no one in the room explodes with anger in response. And as you feel more comfortable voicing your opinions in your personal life, you will gain confidence in expressing them at work also."

"And this will help my mouth heal?" Kevin asked hopefully.

"Certainly. By not holding on to so many negative thoughts and feelings, this area of your body will not be so compromised, and the normal healing processes can occur. You must give yourself permission to be heard."

I gave Kevin an energy treatment, and he left talking about how much lighter he felt. He said that he felt as if he had been released from a straight jacket that he had not known he was wearing. I hoped that he would journal because when we hold things in our heads, we're usually unaware of the assessments that we make about our feelings. Writing things down would help Kevin analyze his thoughts with less fear of repercussions and more compassion for himself.

By talking to my clients and their spirits, I've realized that we often beat ourselves up for even having a thought or feeling that we've declared "wrong." When we do this quick assessment, we may be squelching a line of thinking that has value to us, leading us to our own inner wisdom. In this way, we don't allow ourselves to be seen and heard—by others or even by ourselves. Kevin's situation is not unique. I see clients every week who bite back their healthy responses to avoid rejection, shame, or other negative reactions. Kevin's spirit was giving him a gift in the form of mouth symptoms that were demanding that he take better care of himself emotionally.

Chapter 16

━━━━◦◦◦━━━━

Joey's Perspective

It's June 1st, and my oldest, Joey, has finished his first year of college. The other day he came with me on my morning run with Lola, and I asked him if he'd made any interesting friends over this last semester. He said that he really liked getting to know Brian, a guy from a town that's fifteen miles away from our house.

"Oh, that's close to us," I said. "Did you know him while you were in high school too?"

"No," Joey answered casually. "He didn't go to school nearby because he was in rehab."

"Rehab?" I asked, trying to sound equally casual. "For what?"

"Heroin addiction," Joey said nonchalantly, as if he was telling me that the kid had brown hair.

Thank goodness I was panting while trying to keep up with Joey's long-legged stride so that he didn't notice my mouth fall open. I focused on my running for a moment to keep from stumbling, I was so distracted. I didn't want him to feel defensive, so

I asked gently, "Is he your age? Because that just seems so young to have already been addicted to heroin and gone through rehab. Is he okay now?"

"Yeah, he's good," Joey said. "He's had a really tough life. It's interesting but really sad too. You know, messed up family, lots of fighting, a mom who drinks heavily, that kind of thing. But he's an amazing poet. He writes song lyrics and poetry that could bring you to tears. It doesn't bother you that I'm friends with him does it?"

"No," I assured him, "it doesn't. I think I felt protective of you at first, like it might not be safe for you to hang around kids who might be partying with dangerous stuff, but I trust your judgment, and if you say he's not using anymore, then it's fine. I guess I was just surprised, that's all."

"Yeah, I understand," Joey said. "But I always remember what you told me about people and how they act."

I knew that I needed to stop running before I passed out or threw up (I'm definitely not a long-distance runner), so I slowed to a brisk walk, and Joey fell in step beside me. Only then could I breathe well enough to ask, "What are you talking about?"

Joey smiled at me and said, "Do you remember when I was getting picked on in middle school? By that big kid who loved to push me and a few other kids during PE?"

I nodded my head (still panting), and he continued.

"Well I remember one night at dinner when I was complaining about this kid. Justin and I were talking about what a jerk he was, and how we would love to get him in trouble or humiliate him back.

You said that most people aren't mean at heart and that people act through their pain. So if he was this mean, then he was probably in a lot of emotional pain. You said that maybe his home life was rotten, and that he felt ignored or disempowered there, and so he came to school and took power from other kids to try and feel better."

I was grinning now. "I remember. And you went to school the next day and walked up to him before he pushed you down and said, 'My mom says that you're so mean because you must be hurting a lot. Are you okay? Do you have a bad situation going on at home?'"

Joey jumped in. "Yeah! And he looked flabbergasted and turned bright red and stammered out something like, 'Get away from me, you idiot!' And he never bothered me or my friends again! In fact he went out of his way to avoid us."

"Well, he didn't want to risk you exposing him and his vulnerabilities," I offered. "That wasn't why I told you that—so that you could expose him in front of the other kids. I wanted you to know that people act out their pain so that you didn't take his actions personally, like the abuse was about who you were as a person. I wanted you to have compassion for him at the same time that you felt better about yourself."

"Yeah, I know, but it totally worked! At the time I was just thrilled that you'd taught me a secret about why bullies are bullies. Then I had a way to combat them with words instead of getting into fist fights. Then as I got older, I understood the compassionate part more thoroughly. And as you've taught me more about Buddhism and how to get out of my ego and try to look at things through my heart, I've kept thinking about this stuff. And today I know that everyone is always changing and evolving—you've taught me that too—and so I try to look at someone's past actions as an indicator of what their life was like then. And I think that everyone deserves a clean slate sometimes—a chance to be seen for who they are now instead of what they've done before. Ya' know?"

I smiled with pride. "Yeah, I know," I said as we put Lola in the back of the car and headed for home. Just when you wonder if your kids are really listening.

Chapter 17

Vanessa's Case – Forgiveness Through Understanding

"I'm not sure where to start...," Vanessa said in a soft voice. Vanessa had been referred to me by someone at her church who had discreetly handed her my card when Vanessa revealed that she had recently left her husband of twelve years. I suggested that Vanessa tell me about the type of guidance that she wanted to receive from her spirit.

"Well, I guess I'd like Her help in answering the question that everyone keeps asking me—why did I stay married to Matt for so long? People ask me this all the time—my friends and my family members—and I don't have an answer to give them."

I asked Vanessa why her family and friends were of the opinion that she should have left Matt years ago, and she replied, "Because sometimes he hit me. Not often, but he would shove me and slap me, and if he got really mad, then he'd hit me pretty hard."

I took in a deep, slow breath, focusing on keeping my own reaction neutral. When I hear that a man has beaten his wife, it's easy for me to go to a place of judgment, and I have to work at staying out of that judgmental mindset. I remind myself that each person is being influenced by his own inner suffering, and we hurt others as we push our own emotional discomfort outward when it feels too uncomfortable to contain it. I asked, "Have any of your previous relationships been abusive?"

"No, and that's what's so strange! I grew up in a typical midwestern family outside of Chicago. My dad worked as an architect, and my mom stayed home with us kids. I had a very happy childhood, and so it's not like I came from an abusive background and that's all I knew."

I connected to Vanessa's spirit and She asked Vanessa, *"While you were still living with Matt and friends suggested that you leave him, what thoughts made you stay?"*

Vanessa thought and replied, "I guess I always thought—or hoped—that he would change. That he would care enough about losing me and the kids that he would change. And after we'd have a bad day, he *would* change—for awhile. It's just that the changes never lasted."

"Sometimes," Vanessa's spirit said gently, *"what we desire isn't likely to occur, but we want it so badly that we cling to any small indicators that it will happen. By doing this, we can avoid taking actions that seem scary to us."*

"Like leaving him," Vanessa said quietly.

"Yes, like leaving him."

"Leaving him was the hardest thing I've ever done. And I don't know what I'm going to do next.

My sister has been great—we moved out here to live with her—but I have to get a job, and I don't feel qualified to do anything. I used to be so confident, but now I'm riddled with insecurities, just like the women you hear about who've been abused for years. God, I feel like some pathetic woman in a stereotype! I can't believe I let myself get to this point. I—"

Vanessa's spirit interrupted, *"The first part of your healing journey will consist of understanding enough of your reasons for staying that you can begin forgiving yourself. Forgiving Matt will not be possible until you have begun to forgive yourself."*

"I don't see how I can forgive myself—I feel so stupid! I know that I deserved better than that—the kids did too—and yet I stayed. I used one excuse after another: The kids are in such a good school; I don't want to take them from their father; I have friends in the area..."

Vanessa's spirit gently interrupted, *"Forgiveness comes not just from a decision to forgive, but from possessing enough understanding that you can let go of some of the pain and make room for compassion too."*

Vanessa sighed and nodded for me to go on.

"You're angry at yourself because, in your opinion, you have no basis for tolerating abusive behavior, and therefore, should have had better boundaries with your husband. But the first three relationships that you had in your life (leading up to your marriage) were abusive in their own way. Each relationship was with an increasingly judgmental and angry man, and so the contrast between each relationship

was not extreme. You judge yourself for staying in a relationship that was so vastly different from your upbringing, but in between your childhood and your abusive marriage you developed a habit of trying to love angry men. These men told you that they loved you, and then vented their anger and dissatisfaction with their lives onto you."

"But why did I allow that? Why did I pick these angry men?!" Vanessa cried.

"It's true that your childhood did not include any abuse—you didn't witness abuse or experience it yourself—but you also did not witness many emotionally intense moments between your parents. When they were in front of their children, your parents always appeared to have no disagreements."

Vanessa started to object, but then said, "Yeah, I guess you're right. I remembered them getting frustrated with us, but never at each other. I guess that's not very realistic."

"It left you with no model for what healthy disagreements can look like. So when your first boyfriend blamed you for his bad mood, your inner guidance system was not sure if such blame was appropriate or not, and so you accepted it."

"Well, yes, and because my first boyfriend was older than me and had already had two girlfriends, I thought that he knew what he was doing—with all of his vast experience," Vanessa said sarcastically.

"And so that pattern—to accept responsibility for how your partner felt —became part of your idea of a romantic relationship. And without seeing other couples during their private moments together, you assumed that your relationships were typical, and

private conflict resolution was never really scrutinized.

"*The hostility that your boyfriends showed to you when you were not in public grew increasingly abusive with each successive relationship. But the increases were gradual, and so again, you did not have much conscious awareness of it. But such behavior had an effect on you—it lowered your self-esteem, making you more vulnerable to ever-increasing verbal abuse.*

"*When you met your husband, and the relationship included verbal abuse, your internal guidance system, your radar, did not alert you to anything dangerous. Over the years, your husband conditioned you to accept more responsibility for how he felt and to feel more insecure about your own worth. So by the time the physical abuse happened, you were ready to take on responsibility for that too. Not mentally—mentally you always knew that it was inappropriate—but emotionally, you weren't sure of what kind of treatment you deserved.*"

"I knew that I didn't deserve to be hit!" Vanessa said defensively. "Are You saying that I thought I deserved physical abuse?!"

"*I'm saying that you can know things mentally, but you may not know them emotionally. When we feel, or know, something as our emotional truth, we act on it with certainty. When we have only a mental understanding, we waver, waiting for evidence to make it clear about the action we should take. Mentally, you knew that 'hitting is bad and unacceptable,' but emotionally, you were uncertain of how inappropriate his actions were, and so you were vulnerable to his claims that it was your fault, or that he had a good reason for his behavior.*"

"Then how did I know it emotionally so that I found the courage to leave?"

"Your husband varied his behavior. Do you remember the day that you decided to leave? Not several days later when you actually left, but the Monday night that you decided to leave him?"

"Yes."

"What happened?" her spirit asked.

"He hit me, and when my son, Peter, stepped in to try to stop him, he hit Peter. He had never hit the kids before. In that moment, I left him. In my mind, I divorced him that instant."

"Yes, because you know with certainty—emotionally as well as mentally—that your children did not deserve to be hit because Matt wanted to release his rage on someone. That is an example of knowing something emotionally. Do you see how easy that decision was compared to thinking and trying to decide if you should leave Matt because he hit you?"

Vanessa was quiet for a moment, and I could tell that she was feeling the difference in her body as well as in her mind.

"Yes," she agreed. "I can feel the difference. Once he hit Peter, there was nothing that he or anyone, could've said to make me stay. But before that, when he used to hit me, I would let him talk me into staying and giving him another chance."

"Yes, you were clear that Peter didn't deserve abusive treatment, but less clear about the treatment that you deserved. You knew hitting Peter was inappropriate, and you knew it on every level of your being—mentally, emotionally, and physically."

"Yes! You're right—I felt physically sick when he hit Peter. It was such a violation of how a parent should treat a child."

"So now you understand why you were less clear about the treatment that you deserved and the appropriate behavior between husbands and wives behind closed doors."

Vanessa nodded. She seemed a bit more at peace as she absorbed this information, but her spirit had more to offer.

"There's one more point I want to cover today—the idea of contrast. Every person has a tendency to resist change. The nature of the Universe is impermanence, but people tend to live as if things are permanent, and so change often makes people uneasy.

"When people embrace change, it's frequently because they're so uncomfortable in their current life. In other words, when it gets uncomfortable enough, people push through their resistance to change and move forward in pursuit of more wellbeing. This might be in search of greater physical, mental, or emotional comfort. When people need more peace, they will step off from the place that they know and move into the unknown.

"Because your discomfort with your husband grew in small increments, the contrast was not great enough for you to leave him and venture into the unknown of living as a single parent. But when your husband hit your son, your discomfort was more extreme, and your inner knowing that it was absolutely inappropriate added to the discomfort so that the idea of leaving him was more comfortable than staying with him.

"*Everyone has their contrast point—the point at which the discomfort is so great that it feels like action must be taken, even if that action feels risky. Each person has different contrast points for different subjects.*"

"So that's why most people would have left him as soon as he hit once?" Vanessa asked.

"*Yes, and why some women never leave abusive situations. Many factors go into creating someone's contrast point like their beliefs about themselves and about love/ relationships, and about what's possible in the world. It's important not to judge yourself for your contrast point. If you feel that you would be happier if your contrast point were different, then seek to understand it so that you can modify it.*"

"Well, how do I do that?!" Vanessa asked with a bit of hopelessness to her voice.

"*You're already doing it. You're learning why you tolerated abusive treatment, even though intellectually you understood that it wasn't beneficial or deserved,*" Vanessa's spirit responded patiently.

"But how can I be certain that I won't still tolerate such abuse? Sometimes...sometimes I think about going back to him. I know that I can't—I won't put my kids in harm's way ever again—but there are some things that I miss about him."

"*That is to be expected. If every moment of your life with Matt was terrible, the decision to leave would have occurred much earlier—your contrast point would have been reached quickly. And remembering the pleasant aspects of your marriage does not mean that you will return to your abusive husband—on the contrary, it can help you to better understand why it took so long to reach your contrast point."*

Vanessa looked relieved at the idea that she could think about the pleasant aspects of her marriage without betraying herself or her children. But within a moment, her face looked grave again.

"But what do I do now? I've enrolled the kids in school here, and I'm looking for a job, but I still feel so lost."

"You feel lost because you have made a radical change in your daily living situation, and whenever we make drastic changes to our foundation, we have a period of adjustment. Even if the reason for the change is all positive, as in a desired move to a new house, there is a period of disruption and adjustment while you settle into your new living situation. And your move was not for positive reasons, so you are experiencing feelings of loss, powerlessness, self-doubt, and an understandable fear of the unknown. Be patient and nurturing with yourself during this time of adjustment, just as you have been with your children."

"My sister says that I should meditate, but I've never done that, and I can't imagine getting my brain to turn off for even a second," Vanessa said worriedly.

"Make it your intention to seek peace and greater clarity. Both of these can be gained through periods of quiet reflection. A formal meditation practice need not be started today if that idea feels daunting to you. Perhaps it would be helpful to sit outside and listen to comforting music and just follow your breath. In your mind's eye, watch the air move in and out of your lungs. This will help to center your energy and give your mind something neutral to focus upon. Then

after you've quieted the mind a bit, try journaling. Again, what you write isn't as important as how you feel while you're writing. The more feelings that you can release, the more clarity you can gain. If you notice your mind ruminating, going round and round on one fearful thought, then gently guide yourself to a more empowering thought. The goal is to establish a new state of normal for yourself, where you don't live in fear and carry so much tension in your body."

"Boy, that would be nice!" Vanessa exclaimed.

I gave Vanessa an energy treatment, and we made an appointment for two weeks later so that she'd have time to process all that her spirit had told her and to spend time reflecting and journaling. She left my treatment room looking much more peaceful and confident, and I hoped that she would hold onto those feelings for awhile.

Follow-up:

Vanessa comes in regularly to access her spirit's wisdom as she continues her healing journey. She is learning about the insidious nature of criticism and its ability to lower one's self-esteem. As she learns to forgive herself for staying in an abusive relationship, Vanessa gains confidence in her ability to move forward in new directions. She is slowly gaining confidence in her ability to assess healthy relationships.

Chapter 18

⟞⟝

Encouragement from the Universe

I have to hand it to God/the Universe. Because when I'm starting to doubt my abilities, or how much I really help people, the Universe sends me some encouragement. Lately I've seen several clients who disagreed with parts of the messages that I channeled. I can misunderstand something that I'm hearing from a spirit just as easily as I can misunderstand something that someone tells me over the phone, so I always encourage clients to stop me if I channel something that feels inaccurate. And I know that sometimes when a client disagrees with what I offer, it's because the information feels unsettling, and we all tend to push away statements that feel uncomfortable. But some weeks and some misunderstandings hit me harder, and I find myself questioning the effectiveness of my work. So just when I was getting a bit discouraged, this letter showed up from a client:

Dear Christine,

I saw you recently for a problem I was having with my left ankle, which had started after hiking on some tide pools while on vacation. I was having considerable pain causing me to limp in order to take the pressure off that area. I went to my orthopedic doctor and had several x-rays, which revealed nothing. He suggested that it could be tendonitis and suggested the usual protocol of rest and anti-inflammatory medication. In the ensuing weeks, my ankle did not get better and I continued to limp, sometimes having to use crutches to relieve the pain.

Then a nurse told me about you and I came to see you for a reading. Fairly soon into our session, you looked at my ankle and said, "You have a hairline fracture that was not seen in the x-rays, but it can be seen on an MRI." I was quite impressed by your certainty and because a fracture had been my gut feeling all along, I immediately went back to my doctor and requested an MRI. He arranged for one that afternoon and indeed the MRI showed very clearly that there was a hairline fracture! He put me in a boot and three weeks later I am walking normally, with no pain!

I'm aware that the focus of your work is not diagnostic, but focuses on helping people to understand the emotional stuff that's driving their physical symptoms. You also helped me tremendously in that area in our session, but I have to say, if it weren't for you, I would still be limping and I wanted to express my appreciation!

Thank you,
Claire

I must admit that it's usually fun to figure out medical issues for clients. To me, it's like being handed a puzzle that has stumped others. The Universe's rule seems to be that once a client has pursued the diagnostic tools used in Western medicine and is still suffering, then I'm given information on the issue. Part of my job during a session is to start with what a client understands and expand her knowledge. Usually that means helping her to see the emotional factors that are contributing to her symptoms, but sometimes it means handing her medical information that has yet to be detected.

And there are times when a client's spirit steps forth on Her own, like in the case of this client's, and offers information before I've even asked any questions. This is a part of my job that I really enjoy, and I'm grateful for the reminder today. Another item to list in my gratitude journal tonight!

Chapter 19

"Blending in" at a Cocktail Party

My friend Dana is in town for the weekend, visiting from North Carolina. Like me, Dana left the corporate world to do intuitive work, and we met a couple of years ago when she approached me in Charlotte, North Carolina after I did a public lecture there. She is newer to this work, as she's a mere babe of thirty-something, but she's quite gifted. We enjoy using our gifts to support each other, and we've developed a great friendship.

Last night my friend Maggie invited Dana and me to come along to a cocktail party that she'd been invited to. It was a fund raiser for breast cancer, and some high-profile people (read celebrities, rich people, politicians, and almost-celebrities) would be there. I said yes because I am fond of Mike and Shari, the couple hosting the event, and wanted to support their efforts. We picked up Maggie and headed for the hotel where the event was held. Maggie is a beautiful tall redhead, and Dana is a very striking brunette. Add in my big mop of curly blond hair, and I guess we made a bit of an impression as we walked in. When a few people stared at us, Dana and I quickly became self-conscious while Maggie seemed to shine brighter. Dana and I offered to take our coats to the coat check, and Maggie headed to the bar to get a glass of wine and mingle.

Standing in front of the coat check, Dana and I were chatting about dogs and why people are attracted to particular breeds. Two men walked up and inserted themselves into the conversation, adding their opinions about anyone who owned small "yappy" dogs. When that conversation began to wind down, one of the men asked, "So what do you ladies do for a living?" I've had more years of answering that question, so Dana immediately smiled and looked at me, indicating with her eyes that I was up first. I quickly scanned the energy field of each guy. They had a bit of alcohol in each of them, and consequently, they were fairly open energetically. Since they seemed relaxed and open, I decided to offer the full truth.

"I work as a medical intuitive," I said.

"A what?!" they both asked, almost in unison.

I smiled patiently. "It's okay. Most people don't know what that means. I can see the energy in a person's body, and by using my intuition, I can pick up things about physical symptoms. So I help people increase their awareness about where they hold stress in their body and why." As I finished speaking I could feel several people nearby looking at us and edging in closer. One woman spoke up as she approached us. She was dragging her husband by the arm and clutching her martini with the other.

"Did you say that you're a medical intuitive?" she asked, and before I could answer, "My friend Samantha saw one of those once! She was so dead-on about her!"

I wasn't really sure how to answer that other than, "That's great. I'm glad that she had a good experience."

At this point Josh, one of the two men who had originally approached us, shifted his energy. I could feel him go into his ego, and his attitude shifted from friendly and flirty to challenging. I could feel Dana literally take a half step back, validating what I was sensing.

He thrust his leg towards me and said, "Well what can you tell me about my knee?"

I glanced down at his right pant leg and perceived that his knee was inflamed. When I felt for the emotions in that part of his body, I sensed that he was going through a divorce and was afraid to step into his future because his kids were blaming him for the divorce and were avoiding him. Well I certainly didn't want to share that little piece of information publicly! I'd learned the hard way that even when people say, "Tell me the truth, really!" that they usually aren't ready to publicly share their deepest vulnerabilities. When I do group presentations, I ask for my spirit's help before I select someone whose hand is raised, and She steers me towards the people who have questions that can be safely answered in public. The people who are symptomatic because of something very private (for example they're having an affair) are not called on until they get a sense of how I work, and then usually their hands go down.

I hesitated, unsure what to say in front of this group of strangers. I decided to offer something non-specific. "Well, the right side of the body usually represents your future, so I would say that you're having fears about stepping into your future, and that's causing some inflammation in your knee."

Josh snorted cynically. "That's pretty vague, don't you think? I mean, that sounds like those psychics who say generic stuff that could be true for just about anyone. Want to try again?" and he held his leg out in front of me and dangled it a bit, as if the movement would make things clearer for me. He also closed himself off energetically, similar to when someone is arguing and crosses their arms across their chest and shuts down emotionally. I find that people do this when they want to "test" me. They will ask me to read their energy, but they will subconsciously try to block me from seeing them. It's interesting that we can each do this, considering most people aren't even aware that they are picking up things energetically from others.

Dana knows that I have a smart-ass side and can be tempted to tap into the former lawyer in me to rise up and meet a challenge if I'm not monitoring my ego. She raised her eyebrows and shot me a grin that said, "Go ahead—let him have the truth!"

If this had happened ten years ago, I'm ashamed to admit that I would have taken the bait, and I would have revealed every painful fact that I could pick up on the guy. That's because a decade ago it was more important for me to be right than to be kind. But today I'm more confident in my abilities, and I don't feel the need to prove them to anyone.

And I'm committed to living less from my ego and more from my heart, so I knew that I didn't want to humiliate this guy. But I will admit that it was tempting! Because by now there were five people there with Dana and me, and the woman whose friend had seen a medical intuitive was telling her husband that she wanted to get my card and book a session with me. I tried to quickly think of a way that I could demonstrate what I knew without exposing his personal life to strangers, but I couldn't come up with anything that I felt good about. So I took the high road.

"Well, I could probably get more information if we were somewhere quiet and not public, but not in here."

Josh looked triumphant, and he and his buddy headed off to the bar. The woman and her husband left (surprise—she didn't ask for my card), and the other woman who had been listening disappeared too.

Dana looked at me sympathetically. "Good call. A tough one, but the right choice."

I headed off to the bathroom, and Dana went off to mingle. As I came out of the bathroom, I met up with Maggie who seemed excited.

"I've been looking for you!" She said rapidly. "You've got to come meet this guy Rob. He's so hunky, and he's a doctor!"

Maggie led me towards a small banquet room where items were being auctioned off for the charity. In front of the room was a small bar, and standing in front of the bar was indeed a hunky guy. Maggie introduced me to Rob, and the three of us talked for a moment. He was very articulate and funny, which is always enjoyable, but something was making my radar go off. Since his conversation wasn't giving me any clues, I shifted my focus to look at his energy. His energy looked...tangled. Like a ball of spaghetti that couldn't easily be separated. About ten minutes later, Rob excused himself to say hello to a friend, and Maggie immediately turned to me and said, "Well?! What do you think? Isn't he awesome?"

I hesitated. "Well, he seems great..."

"Uh-oh!" Maggie groaned. "What's wrong with him? Is he dying? Is he gay? Is he a bank robber?"

"No, no, and no!" I said. "It's just that his energy seems tangled up."

Maggie brightened. "Well, that's okay, I'm a big tangled mess sometimes too. Maybe he's just having a crazy week at work."

"Yeah, I don't think that's it. The energy feels feminine. I think that he's really involved with someone already. Like, he may be married or living with someone—*that* kind of involved." I looked at Maggie sympathetically.

"Well, I certainly hope not! He just asked me out and I said yes! And he's not wearing a wedding ring—I looked for that. You might be wrong—that happens sometimes, right?"

I smiled encouragingly. "Absolutely. No one's right all the time, and I could certainly be off-base here."

Then Maggie's eyes opened wide. "Hey, I know! Just connect to his spirit and ask if he's dating anyone."

"I can't," I said. "I don't connect to anyone's spirit without their permission. That's a total invasion of a person's privacy."

Maggie looked desperate. "C'mon! I'm not asking you to look at his tax returns and tell me what he made last year. I just want to know if he's dating someone!"

I had another idea. "I won't break the honor code that I have with the spirit world, but I will go find the party host and see what he can tell us about Rob." This seemed to appease Maggie, and I walked away just as Rob was returning from the bathroom. I looked at him as I passed by him, and yep, some woman's energy was still all wrapped around him, and it wasn't Maggie's energy.

I found Mike near the stage where Sheryl Crow had just performed. I pulled him aside and discreetly pointed at Rob.

"Do you know him?" I asked.

"Rob? Yeah, he's a good guy—and a great dentist. He got my kids over their fear of the dentist chair. You should try him if you're looking for a good dentist."

"Okay, thanks." I said. "I think that my friend Maggie is hitting it off with him. Please tell me that he's not married."

Mike was distracted, but as he looked away said, "Um, I don't think he's married right now. He and his wife have split up and gotten back together several times over the last two years, so I'm not sure where that stands. But he's a great dentist —you should try him." That last statement was thrown over his shoulder as he rushed to block a bus boy who was trying to hug Sheryl Crow as she came off the stage.

Sigh. I didn't relish reporting this news to Maggie, but I also knew that she would want to know the truth. Being intuitive wasn't feeling super rewarding that night. I relayed the information to Maggie, who was disappointed but luckily did not shoot the messenger. She went off to find Rob and ask him some direct questions.

Not surprisingly, Maggie elected to cancel her date with Rob. He admitted that things were not completely settled with his ex-wife and then proceeded to talk about the end of his marriage until Maggie signaled for Dana and me to come and rescue her from the conversation.

Chapter 20

Kevin's Follow-Up Session – Distilling His Truth

I t had been two and a half weeks since Kevin had come for his first session. When he arrived he looked a bit frazzled—mentally confused and emotionally drained. He sat down on the sofa in my treatment room, and I noticed that his perfect posture was absent. He appeared a bit defeated, shoulders slumped and chest caved in rather than puffed out. I immediately sent compassionate energy towards him, and I watched his chest muscles react slightly as the energy was received. Kevin didn't yet seem to feel the difference emotionally, but I trusted that he would begin feeling better once we began our work.

I asked Kevin how he'd been feeling since our first session.

"Well, when I left here, I felt great, but it didn't last. Two days later I spoke up and told my girlfriend about something that pissed me off, and then she didn't speak to me for two days! I thought that my spirit said that everyone wouldn't react like my dad did, but that sure felt like my dad!"

I knew better than to try and address those events myself, so I connected to Kevin's spirit so that Kevin could ask Him his questions. Kevin's spirit was ready with a response.

"Kevin did a great job of listening during his first session and of absorbing some very important information, but he has not taken the advice to journal first and then speak his truth. It can feel cumbersome to proceed this way, but it is necessary. Because Kevin has suppressed his opinions for so many years, he is not well connected to his own truth. There is an initial reaction on the emotional level, but it is difficult for him to know exactly why he is upset. So his comments may seem overly harsh or non-specific, because he is not well practiced in expressing himself.

"Likewise, the people in Kevin's life are generally not used to him speaking up and offering a differing perspective, and so they may not always react well to his comments.

"Kevin's girlfriend, Sarah, wasn't upset because Kevin had voiced his opinion, but because he'd made blanket statements about her and her habits."

I paused here and opened my eyes to look at Kevin for confirmation of that statement.

"Yeah, He's probably right about that," Kevin agreed halfheartedly. "I told her that she always complains about her weight, but then she eats fattening sweets like cheesecake and cookies. It's pretty simple, I told her—if you want to lose weight, quit eating all that junk food. She got mad, started to yell, and then looked like she was going to cry. Then she barely said two words to me for the next two days. So...expressing that truth didn't get me very far."

Kevin's spirit began talking even before Kevin had finished his last sentence. *"But is that your truth? Or is it a judgment? Before you answer, please take a moment and say out loud what you would write in a journal if one were placed before you right now."*

"Okay...," Kevin seemed unsure, but warmed to the idea quickly. "Okay, here's what I would write. I would say that she always does this; she goes through these periods of eating fattening foods when she comes home from work. Then she complains the next day about feeling fat. Then after awhile—maybe a few days or a week—she goes back to eating healthy and ignoring the junk food. I don't know why she does that. She knows that she will be miserable about the extra pounds that she puts on!"

"This is the first bit—please continue," Kevin's spirit encouraged.

"Hmmm... Well, like I said, these binges seem to come and go. I guess they correspond to when things are bad at work. No! They correspond to when she has difficult conversations with her mother or her brother. They both tend to lean on her for advice, and then when things don't work out, they blame her. She feels trapped by them and doesn't know how to tell them to run their own lives."

Kevin got quiet for a moment, and I waited for the lightbulb moment. I didn't have to wait long.

"Oh! I just had a thought. I think that she goes for that junk food when she's feeling frustrated with her family situation. She can't change them, so she looks for comfort somewhere else."

Kevin's spirit smiled. *"Yes, she does. And so now I ask you to see that your initial reaction—and your statement to Sarah—was not your truth, but your reaction to a frustrating dynamic you were witnessing. Your truth is that you wish that Sarah did not have to feel such stress from her family that she feels the need to seek comfort from unhealthy food. If you had gotten in touch with this understanding, then your comments to her would have felt more like loving support and less like criticism. You could have suggested that she come to you and talk about her feelings of frustration rather than try to use food to stuff her feelings of powerlessness. I'm confident that if you had presented her with your truth as you now understand it, you would have received a better response."*

Kevin nodded his head in agreement. "Yeah, that feels really different than the energy that I hit her with when I was so frustrated. Wow, I feel terrible now! I wish I could have said this stuff to her instead."

I explained that there is a learning curve, and that the exercise was to help him see the value in journaling before he tries to offer his truth to others. We talked about the difference between an initial negative reaction, which lets him know that something is off, and his actual truth, which may take some time to uncover. I told him that one way to speed up his learning process is to bring examples into his sessions so that his spirit can help him uncover his truth.

Kevin brightened. "Okay, then here is another situation. My dad is a yeller, right? Now that I'm an adult, he doesn't really yell at me anymore, but he still yells at my mom and talks to her like she's stupid. It really bugs me, but I'm not sure what to say to him. What do you think I should say to him, and should I say something when he's yelling at her, or later when things have calmed down?"

I knew that I was dealing with a potentially explosive family dynamic, so I didn't even try to answer Kevin's questions myself. Luckily his spirit stepped forward to offer wise guidance.

"First I advise you to get clear that your dad's treatment of your mom is not your issue to fix. Both of your parents participate in that relationship and the unhealthy dynamics within it, and you are not a part of that relationship. So it's not recommended that you speak to either of them with the intent of correcting their bad behavior.

"What you are encouraged to speak about is how their behavior affects you. Speaking your truth means commenting on how something feels in your heart, not simply labeling behavior as good or bad. People are usually willing to listen to your comments about how something makes you feel, but are not open to hearing your judgments of them."

Kevin held up his hand to stop me. "Wait! How is their relationship not my business?! They're my parents, and if spending time around them is torturous, why can't I say that?"

"It is fine to speak of how their behavior makes you feel, but it is not advisable to speak about how your dad's behavior makes your mother feel. Those

are her feelings to express."

"But she won't say anything! Which is why he still talks to her that way."

"Your mother has learning to do, just as you have your own journey with its lessons. The best way to help your mother is not by trying to make healthy boundaries between her and your father, but to make healthy boundaries for yourself, and let her observe your new boundaries."

Kevin's shoulders drooped. "I'm not really following You here."

"For example, one boundary that you can establish is that you don't want to be around your parents if your dad is berating your mom. You can express this new boundary when things are calm between them, and explain that when they argue, or when your dad is aggressively criticizing your mother, it is uncomfortable to be around, and so if it occurs in your presence, you will leave the house."

"Whoo–hoo! My dad would look at me like I was nuts if I said that! And then he would probably ask me why I was being such a pansy."

"And is it 'being a pansy' to not wish to be around someone who is being unkind to someone you love?"

Kevin brightened and sat up straighter. "No, it isn't! Thank you—that's a good point."

"The lack of boundaries between you and your father exists because he requires that the people close to him accept his definition of appropriate. Your mother did, and so as a child, you came to understand that his perception of himself was the only correct one.

"But as an adult, it is healthy for you to give

yourself permission to question his decisions and to feel in your heart what feels healthy and appropriate to you. And as you do so, it encourages your mother to feel out her own truth as well. Your father will not like that you disagree with his definitions of acceptable behavior, but it is unlikely that he will completely abandon his relationship with you."

"And what if he does? What if he disowns me and refuses to speak to me again?"

"While that is unlikely, it is possible. So you will need to decide if keeping your father in your life is important enough to live by his definitions of honorable behavior instead of your own. But as you continue exploring your own truth and recognizing what feels honoring to you and the people you love, it will probably get more and more difficult to be in the presence of someone who is dishonoring."

"And that discomfort is a good thing?"

"Yes, because as you strengthen the emotional connection that you have to yourself, you can more quickly get clarity about what is healthy for you. The physical symptoms that you have in your mouth have stemmed from a vague sense that something was unhealthy for you, but because you lacked clarity about how or why it was inappropriate, you stopped yourself from speaking.

"Ideally, your emotional discomfort alerts you to the fact that something is not quite right. And then your connection to your heart/feelings, combined with your courage to honor what feels healthy to you, gives you the determination to discover your truth and then to act on it."

"Whew. This is intense stuff. Just the thought of

confronting my dad makes me get a tight stomach and a dry mouth."

"This is understandable because part of your definition of yourself is someone who is loyal and doesn't contradict the leader."

"Yeah, I guess that's true."

"But is that still the best way for you to be in the world? Such behaviors served you well while you were in the military, but perhaps now such actions block you from honoring yourself in your current relationships."

"I know that you're right—I mean that my spirit is right. I think that sometimes I know that someone's behavior is ridiculous, but I duck away from confronting him because I don't want the conflict."

"Yes, and again we can look to your childhood where questioning your dad's perceptions and decisions led to you being punished and shamed. Shame is very effective in squashing someone's desire to question authority. You are encouraged not to judge yourself as cowardly in the face of personal confrontation, but as inexperienced. You have very few instances where you have disagreed with an authority figure like your father or your boss and felt positive about the conversation afterwards. Both of these men engage in behavior that is rather bullying as they strive to discourage people from disagreeing with them.

"It is difficult to practice speaking your truth to such men, which is why you are encouraged to journal first so that you are clear about your truth. And then you must summon your courage and decide that being honest and establishing healthy

boundaries is more important than maintaining an unhealthy, tense relationship.

"Recognize that in order to remain in such relationships, you have agreed to give up much of your personal power to these men. Here's a tip: If you feel disempowered when in the room with someone, you probably do not have a healthy relationship where both parties are respecting one another."

"Well, then...shoot! There are several relationships where I feel disempowered all the time! Okay, I'm going to change this. And not just for the sake of healing my mouth, but so that I can feel more comfortable in my own skin."

"Excellent!" I said quickly, wanting to solidify this new determination to honor himself. "And remember that these changes don't need to happen immediately. Sometimes once we see that things need changing in a relationship, we can't not see it—everywhere we look, it's in our face. But your relationships took a long time to get to this place, and you can't completely remodel them today. Just commit to continually figuring out what your truth is, and then know that you will make boundaries based on your new understandings."

Kevin looked almost radiant with confidence and clarity, so I continued.

"And journaling is going to be a vitally important tool for you. So get a notebook—maybe a few—and have them in your car and at your desk so that you can quickly access this process of getting to your truth."

Kevin chuckled and shook his head in disbelief.

I looked at him questioningly, and he offered an explanation.

"When I came home from running errands yesterday, I discovered a spiral-bound notebook in one of my bags from the office-supply store. I didn't buy it, but there it was listed on the receipt, so I had paid for it without realizing it. I was a bit frustrated, but it only cost a couple of dollars, so it wasn't worth driving back to the store to return it. I tossed it onto a pile of stuff on the end of my desk. Now I think my spirit and the Universe conspired to have that notebook come home with me somehow!"

I told him that small miracles happen all the time, and once we start looking for them, we really begin seeing them. Sometimes I become cynical, and then I don't notice them for awhile. When I open back up to their presence, I notice that I feel more looked after and less on my own. Since I like that feeling, I try to keep looking for this evidence that the Universe is always conspiring to help me.

I gave Kevin an energy treatment, and before he left, he booked his next appointment, adding that he would bring his notebook with him to get more advice on how to deal with the revelations that he uncovered through his writing.

Follow-up:

Kevin's mouth has continually improved, and his dentist now considers both auto-immune conditions to be almost completely healed. Kevin has learned that when he holds back and doesn't speak his truth, his mouth will get very dry and sensitive.

This is his cue to get quiet and journal in order to discover his true feelings. He is still working on how he presents his truth to others but is getting continually more skillful. He has been pleasantly surprised at his ability to successfully renegotiate the power structure of his relationships.

Chapter 21

———◦◦◦———

Becky's Case – A Celebrity Alone in a Crowd

My new client is already twenty minutes late when her assistant calls to say that she's running late. No kidding. I'm hoping that this client won't be more evidence that the clichés about celebrities are based in truth. The typical celebrity clients are usually surprised by me because I speak truthfully to all my clients, and famous people are frequently surrounded by people who only tell them what they want to hear. This prevents them from getting balanced feedback on themselves, and so when they receive it from me, they're either grateful or really pissed off.

I knew that this client, Becky, was bringing her assistant with her, but I wasn't prepared for what happened when I opened my front door—and neither was my dog, Lola. As the door opened, three small dogs came running into the house. Two were French bulldogs, and one was a chihuahua. They jumped at my legs for a second until they noticed Lola standing behind me. They immediately abandoned me and lurched at Lola, climbing up the front of her as if she were a piece of playground equipment. Lola is very polite, so she stood still for this behavior so as not to hurt the dogs, but with a French bulldog hanging off her ear, she looked at me with an expression that said, "What the hell?!" I rushed to her defense, scooping up the small dogs and tucking one under each arm. I picked up the third one and stood up to hand it to the assistant when I noticed that there were three people in my foyer.

Becky introduced her two companions as her personal assistant and her dog trainer. Already unimpressed with the dog trainer, I handed her the third dog and asked her if she had leashes for them so that they didn't run through the house chewing on things (the one in my left hand was already gnawing on my sleeve). When she held up three leashes, I raised my eyebrows to indicate that those would be more useful if they were actually attached to the dogs. I helped her put them on, then pointed her back outside and told her that she was welcome to walk the dogs around the neighborhood for the next hour. Having three puppies and this trainer in my treatment room would make for a very distracting session.

With the (alleged) dog trainer disposed of, we were down to Becky and her assistant. Becky asked if her assistant could come into the session to take notes for her. I normally don't mind if someone brings a friend or family member along for a session, but my intuition told me that this session would be most effective if done in private, so I suggested that Becky tape the session using her cell phone instead. This rendered the assistant unnecessary, and I suggested a local coffee shop where she could spend the next hour.

As I closed the door on the last of Becky's entourage, I turned to Becky and saw that she looked rather lost and small. Which was interesting, because this woman is a powerhouse on stage. I ushered her into my treatment room, and we got started. Becky said that she wanted a session with me in order to get guidance from her spirit on her sleep issues. She also said that she wanted some input on the subject of romantic relationships. I asked her how many relationships she'd had in her 27 years, and she said "many." When asked if there was a pattern that she noticed in them, she said that men tended to get possessive of her, and then the relationship would end. When she used the word "possessive," I could feel Becky's spirit step back to indicate that She disagreed with that statement. That peaked my interest, and so I closed my eyes and connected to Becky's spirit.

Silently I asked, "Why do You disagree with Becky's use of the word 'possessive'?"

Her spirit replied, *"Because the most common complaint among the men that she has dated is 'lack of privacy.' Becky keeps herself surrounded by others, and so she misses out on experiencing true intimacy with one person."*

I relayed this message to Becky, who pondered it for a moment before saying, "But I like people! I love having lots of people around. Is that a bad thing?"

Becky's spirit responded, *"It's not as simple as labeling it good or bad. What's important is to understand your motivations behind never wanting to be alone."*

"Oh yeah, I hate being alone! From the time I was 9 years old, I was working on films. And when you're working on a film, you have this huge family—the cast and crew all live together on location and hang out together. My parents were really trusting—too trusting—of the people involved, and so I had relatively little supervision from them. I had a chaperone of course because they didn't want me getting mixed up with drugs or alcohol, but that also meant that I was never alone unless I was sleeping or showering. During the day, there were assistants to go over my lines with me, to do my hair and makeup, and to help me answer fan mail and stuff. So I just got used to being surrounded by people."

Becky's spirit offered, *"And you got used to receiving positive feedback almost constantly. The people that were on your payroll were there to help you stay happy and focused on your work. You didn't have a chance to develop your ability to discern how you truly felt about things. Instead you came to rely on the feedback from everyone around you."*

"Maybe...but I think that I make decisions on my own too! I know what I like when I shop for clothes, and shoes, and—"

"Do you ever shop alone?" her spirit asked.

"Well...no. But it's more fun to shop with friends."

Becky's spirit suggested that perhaps Becky uses the people around her to narrow down her options and then chooses her opinion from the various ones offered. Becky considered this for a moment.

"Maybe I do that, I'm not sure. But why is that bad?"

"Again, it's not about good or bad, just understanding how your current lifestyle affects your relationships. For example, if your various friends and employees have differing opinions about a man that you are dating, how does this impact your feelings for him?"

"Well...I guess it did make it confusing when my hairdresser liked Brian, the last guy I dated, but my makeup artist Sandy—she's a great friend—said that she didn't trust him."

"And the problem with each of these opinions is that they were based on relatively small amounts of time spent with Brian and on how each of those people felt about relationships in general. How did you feel about Brian? What was your opinion of him?"

"Well, he was a lot of fun, but then he seemed so possessive, wanting to go off away from everyone all the time. I thought that because he was famous too that, he would be used to rooms full of people, but he didn't like it. And then my friends felt like he was a drag, always breaking up the party to send everyone home so that we could be alone. So...I don't know—I liked some things about him, but then there were some things that my friends were right about, so...I don't really know. But that's not my friends' fault!" she said defensively.

I decided to switch subjects and come back to romantic relationships later. When asked about her sleep issues, Becky said that once she fell asleep, she was alright, but sometimes it could take her as long as four hours to fall asleep. She had taken prescription drugs to help her sleep but had discontinued them due to unpleasant side effects. She described a restless mind, racing from one subject to another and unable to quiet down.

Becky's spirit offered some insight into the situation. *"You live in a culture that surrounds you with stimulation from electronic devices every moment of the day. Between your computer and your cell phone, you are never out of contact with others. And in your situation, you're also surrounded by many people each moment of the day. The amount of stimulation sent to your brain in each moment is staggering. Then when you lie down to go to sleep, it is like going into an isolation chamber because the contrast is so great between the bombardment of stimulation during the day and the lack of stimulation at night."*

"Wow! That makes so much sense! I'm always answering questions and either texting or talking on the phone. I have two cell phones—one personal and one business—and it seems like someone is always handing me one of them or asking me the answer to a texted question. Because everyone is so nice to me, and I'm so grateful for the movie roles that I keep getting, I never want to complain, but sometimes I want to go hide in the bathroom for awhile!"

Becky's spirit helped her to see that what she needed was a wind-down period, where her brain could cycle down the amount of stimulation it was receiving and responding to. An hour before bedtime, her spirit suggested that she turn off her cell phones and computers and give her brain one thing to focus on, such as listening to music or reading a book. Even watching television would suffice if she picked one relatively calm show and didn't channel surf during commercials. Then twenty minutes before turning out the light, Becky was encouraged to journal, emptying out of her mind all the unfinished business that was occupying her thoughts and listing items that were on her "to-do" list for the next day. With her brain less charged and her mind feeling less pressure to remember or resolve things, hopefully Becky would be better able to fall asleep.

With the sleep issue addressed, Becky seemed more relaxed and open, so I returned to the subject of dating and relationships.

I asked, "Can you remember a guy that you dated that you enjoyed but the people around you seemed to disapprove of?"

Becky thought for a moment and then smiled. "Yeah, Gabe." As she said his name, the energy in front of her heart chakra glowed bright pink—a good sign since that color indicates positive emotions.

"Why did you enjoy him so much, and why do you think your friends and employees didn't like him?"

It was interesting to watch Becky struggle to answer that question as it meant sorting out her truth from the opinions of those she surrounded herself with. "Umm, I think that they didn't like him because he was sort of shy and didn't like to be in big groups of people. They called him a 'buzz-kill' because when he showed up, I usually left with him pretty soon afterwards."

"Okay, and what did you like about him?" I asked.

"He made me feel...safe and special. Does that

sound dumb? I mean I'm never unsafe, I guess."

Becky's spirit offered some help. *"It seemed that he made you feel emotionally safe. Because he was very nonjudgmental and seemed to require no more from you than just being together, you were able to just relax and not worry about pleasing or impressing others."*

"Yes! That's it! He was so sweet, and just... comfortable to be around—when we were alone. But when we were with lots of other people, he got very quiet, and I could tell he hated it."

Becky's spirit asked, *"Do you feel that your friends every really got to know Gabe?"*

"No, not really. In hindsight, I probably should have had him spend time with each of them one by one, or at least not as a big group, so that they could've seen how sweet he was."

"So perhaps their reactions were not a reflection of who Gabe was, but on how Gabe's presence meant that their party would soon be over because you would be leaving."

Becky looked irritated. "Wow—that makes me feel like they're all pretty selfish."

"The suggestion was not meant to make you resent your friends and employees, but to point out that their motivations for liking who you date have a lot to do with how that man impacts their lives. This is important to notice since you have a habit of asking for your friends' input to help you assess the men in your life."

"Sh**! I feel like I need to run after Gabe and try to get him back."

I held up my hand. "Wait, Becky, this isn't just about Gabe. Your spirit is trying to help you see that it's not advisable to weigh other people's opinions more heavily than your own since each person has her own perspective and is pursuing her own goals. To discover your own truth, you may want to listen to other perspectives, but in the end, you'll need to tune in to your own inner feelings. And doing that means separating yourself from your entourage long enough to explore your own feelings."

The look on Becky's face told me that she was having an "ah-ha" moment. One of the best parts of my job is getting to be present when clients have these great moments of understanding and their lives shift along with their perspective.

"Now I see the pattern! The guys that I liked the most were special because they wanted to just spend time hanging out with me alone, and when my friends labeled that as being possessive, it was because they didn't like having to give up time with me. And I had such a negative association with that word 'possessive'—my aunt used to call my uncle possessive because he never liked her to leave the house without him—that when I heard that label, I usually dumped the guy. So I don't have a problem with men, I have a problem with my so-called friends!"

Becky's spirit spoke gently, *"Perhaps it's best not to see it as a problem, but as a clearer understanding. Now that you see the value in spending time alone—to get clear on your truth about people and situations— you will arrange to spend less time surrounded by people who are motivated by their own agendas. It's always wise to double-check your perspective by gathering input from a few trusted people, but it's even more important to sit quietly and feel what your own heart is telling you."*

Becky sat still for a moment, and I suspected that she was going back through her mind and listing all the men that she had dumped without understanding her own feelings about them.

"Wow, this is big stuff, isn't it?" she finally said. "I really need to develop my own opinions about things and then feel comfortable expressing them. And I need to have people around me who really hear me, not who just say what I want to hear and then try to manipulate my opinion later."

Success! Becky's spirit gave her a few more tips on getting centered in her true feelings through journaling and separating herself from others, and I recommended a supplement (the flower essence made from a Walnut tree) to help her hold herself energetically separate from others. She left my house looking much stronger and calmer than the flustered woman who had appeared on my doorstep an hour earlier.

Follow-up:

When I spoke to Becky two months later at a cocktail party, she reported that on the nights that she followed her spirit's suggestions, she drifted off to sleep within fifteen minutes of turning out the light! She then confessed that she only followed this protocol about three nights a week, but that she felt empowered because she now understood the cause of her insomnia.

Becky comes in periodically for a session when she's in town filming or between movie projects. Her spirit has helped her learn to assess the healthiness of a romantic partner by listening to input from friends but then feeling her own heart's desires. She is learning to enjoy time alone without feeling guilty that she's abandoning her entourage. I can see this difference in her acting. As she has developed the capacity to sit in stillness, she has deepened the emotional intensity that she can convey on screen.

Chapter 22

The Joys of Parenting – Resolving Bickering

Last night I was talking to my friend Sandy on the phone. Sandy lives in North Carolina, where I work several months out of each year, and we talk nearly every day. We've been friends for years and are loyal and supportive of each other like sisters. When the conversation turned to my writing of this book, I told Sandy that I was including chapters about raising the boys. She immediately said, "You should tell the story of when you and I took the boys to the Biltmore Estate in Asheville."

I went blank. "I remember us all going, but I don't remember anything significant happening there that I would write about. What am I forgetting?"

Sandy laughed. "That's just it. It was something so natural for you that it doesn't stand out in your memory. But it sure stands out in mine!"

As Sandy recalled the episode, I remembered it, especially her reaction afterwards. Since she's a very wise friend, I'm taking her suggestion to include this anecdote.

Justin and Joey were 14 and 16, and I had brought them with me to North Carolina during the summer of 2012. Because we used to live on a beautiful lake north of Charlotte, North Carolina, the boys have friends in the area and fond memories too, and they love visiting each summer. But they are typical siblings, getting on each other's nerves periodically and inflicting that misery on the adults nearby. Sandy and I had taken the boys to tour the gorgeous Biltmore Estate in Asheville and were having a lovely time touring the house and grounds of the estate. Or at least it was lovely until the boys began bickering.

If you have kids, or if you grew up with siblings, you know that once bickering begins, it's a torturous process of each child trying to demonstrate that the other kid is worse—a bigger fool, a meaner person, a stupid idiot, etc. Traditional parenting of such activities usually looks like me saying, "Boys, knock it off. Be nice to each other." In my experience, this request is as effective as tossing a raisin at the situation. It bounces off the boys, and they look at me confused then resume their bickering and put-downs.

The bickering began when we sat down at a café on the estate grounds to have some lunch and continued for about twenty minutes. Then I hit my limit. I started to fuss at them, telling them how I was disappointed that their pettiness was ruining a nice afternoon, when I noticed their energy. Both of them had energy in the stomach area, and it was moving in a way that indicated that they were each feeling insecure. Apparently the barbs that each of them had thrown had found their mark, and they had successfully made the other person feel "less than." I decided to approach this situation from a different angle—my perspective.

"Hey guys. I know that sometimes you roll your eyes when I talk about your energy, but I want to share what I'm seeing. Both of you are really in your egos right now. Your words are effective if your goal is to hurt the other one, but I don't see this situation going anywhere good. Remember when you were young, and you would fight and I would send you to your rooms? Not to punish you but to shift from your ego into your heart. Do you remember?"

They both looked a bit annoyed with me but grumbled a "yeah." Then Joey said, "Well, it's going to be a bit difficult to send us to our rooms right now!" Justin snickered in agreement.

"I know, I know," I said. "But even when you were little guys, you could go into your rooms and listen to music, or read, or meditate, and then once you'd shifted from that angry place to a calm, heart-centered place then you would come out of your room and apologize to each other. And not because I made you apologize. My rule was just that you couldn't come out of your room until you could feel that your energy was in your heart. The great thing was that once you shifted to that perspective, you saw the other person's point of view to some degree and you no longer wanted to crush his feelings and prove that you were right or were the better kid. Do you remember?"

Both boys nodded. They weren't thrilled with my speech, but they remembered the approach that

I'd frequently used when I was tired of refereeing their arguments.

"Well, I'm going to ask you both for a favor. Take a moment and see if you can shift your focus. Imagine pulling your energy up to the center of your chest. You're older now, and I don't have to send you to your room or wait for thirty minutes for you to accomplish this change. Just close your eyes and take a deep breath and do it."

"Mom!" they both groaned in unison. "We don't want to sit here in a restaurant with our eyes closed! We'll look stupid!"

I wasn't backing down. "Then put your menus up in front of you. But I'm pulling the mom card here and saying 'Do it!' If you can bicker in public, then you can do this too."

I handed each of them a big menu, and they disappeared for several minutes. Sandy looked at me with wide eyes but said nothing.

When they put their menus down and looked at me, I said, "Okay. Let's try this: I'd like each of you to show some accountability. Tell your brother why you said something, or how you helped make things worse between you."

Joey went first. "Well, I guess when Justin made a crack about me out by the rose garden, I felt like he didn't respect me, and so I was punishing him for it. But I should have just told him that he was making me feel bad instead of trying to make him feel bad too because that obviously wasn't fixing things between us."

Then Justin spoke. "I'm sorry that I made you feel bad out there. I was just trying to be funny. I didn't think that I was putting you down."

Joey's energy flared red as he got defensive. "How could I not get defensive when you say stupid things like—"

I held up my hand. "Wait a minute! Feel the difference now. When you get angry, it feels agitated and uncomfortable, right?" Joey nodded his head. "Stay out of that energy. Be determined to stay in your heart so that your perspective stays calm and gentle. You just heard your brother say that his intention was to be funny, and not at your expense. This is where his motives have to be given more weight than how you interpreted his words. Okay?"

Joey sat still for a moment, considering what I'd just said. Then he took a deep breath and exhaled. "Okay. I get that you were trying to be funny. And once I felt hurt I wanted to humiliate you using *my* humor. Truce?"

Justin smiled at his brother. "Sure, truce. Hey, we should tell Sandy that funny story about the kid we saw by the water fountain!" And harmony was restored.

A little while later, we visited the gift shop before we headed home. The boys found a rack of funny cards and were laughing together. Sandy and I wandered over to a jewelry counter. I could feel that Sandy felt a bit "off," and I looked at her energy to figure out why. Her energy was moving in a way that suggested that she was confused and processing some information. "Are you okay?" I asked. "Is there something that you're trying to figure out?"

She grinned at me and said, "I forget sometimes that you notice so much!"

"I don't mean to pry," I said quickly.

"No, I don't mean that. I can feel you being concerned, not nosy. I was just standing here thinking about what happened at lunch and wondering what my life would have been like if I'd been parented in the way that you're parenting the boys. I know that sometimes you think that you're raising them like most parents do when you feel like you're always nagging them about homework and chores. But moments like that, when you teach them a peaceful way to end squabbles and understand the power of shifting their perspective—those moments are going to have a profound impact on their lives."

I considered what Sandy had said. I had always asked the boys to understand their own motives and be responsible for their energy, so I hadn't really thought about how unique that parenting style was. I thanked Sandy for pointing that out to me and had a moment of appreciation, basking in the experience of a successful parenting moment. Not five minutes later I heard the store clerk scolding my boys for playing with a ball in the store—a reasonable objection since there were breakables everywhere.

"Boys!" I tried to yell and keep my voice down at the same time. "Get over here!" They were laughing as we left the store and remarking that it wasn't too smart to sell balls in a store that also sold glassware. I had to grin. I much preferred them being united and happy, even if it meant beating a hasty retreat out of a gift store.

Chapter 23

⊸∘⊂⊘∘⊂

Paula's Case – When Is a Marriage Over?

Paula is similar to many of my clients in that she began seeing me for help with her physical symptoms and continued booking sessions long after we healed those symptoms. Once clients experience talking with their spirit and receiving that guidance, they come back when things in their life feel out of balance or troubling. Paula has two children: Monica is 11 and Derek is 14. Paula works part-time at a local clothing store owned by her friend and is home with her children most of the time.

Paula is married to George, and their marriage is not in great shape. They have been together for nearly twenty-five years, and they seem bored with each other and intolerant of their differences. Paula is kind and gentle with others, but with her husband, she is impatient and judgmental. She is convinced that her behavior is in reaction to George's treatment of her and tells me stories of his nasty comments that are made in front of their children.

Today when I opened my door, Paula looked

defeated and teary-eyed. When she sat down, she described another hostile exchange between her and her husband, ending with her son taking George's side and telling Paula, "Don't be such a nag, Mom! Leave Dad alone!" Instead of telling his son to stay out of the conversation, George smiled triumphantly and left the room with Derek in tow. This prompted her daughter, Monica, to rush to her defense, and Paula was miserable with the teams that seemed to be forming.

Paula concluded, "Honestly, Christine, I don't know what to do. George refuses to go to therapy because he says that I'm the problem not him, so why should he have to go. So I feel like I have to endure this until Monica leaves for college, and then I can file for divorce."

I couldn't imagine how they could stay together for that many years with so much anger between them. I asked Paula, "Do you think that you can remain in this relationship for six more years?"

"What choice do I have?" wailed Paula. "I mean, I know that I have a choice, but in my mind, I really don't. My parents divorced when I was in elementary school, and it was horrible! I remember them fighting about me and my sister and whose turn it was to have us for each holiday. I can't do that to my kids. If I can just find a way to hold it together for six years, then I can have my freedom."

I know when it's time to turn over the microphone to someone much wiser than myself, so I closed my eyes and connected to Paula's spirit. The energy I felt let me know that I had to slow down so we could approach this topic gingerly.

"When raising children, it's important to provide them with a loving, serene family life. But when that does not exist because the husband and wife do not have a healthy relationship, the parents should consider the best way that they can create a calm, supportive home.

"Because so much of the focus for Paula and her husband George has been on how to control the other person, the quality of life that they have all been living has suffered. There is a constant power struggle between George and Paula, as they each want to prove that the other is more to blame for the unhappy relationship that exists. The children have begun to mimic this tension and quarrel with each other frequently."

"But wait a minute—don't all kids argue?" Paula asked defensively.

"Absolutely—all people argue. But your children have begun arguing about who is more right, more worthy, more valid. This is a behavior pattern that they are learning from observing their parents. What they have concluded—on the subconscious level—is that if one person is better than the other, then that individual gets more power in the relationship. So there is a constant struggle to convince the other person that he or she is less intelligent, less caring, and less lovable. This is a pattern that each of them will most likely take into their romantic relationships in the future. Because such behavior undermines healthy relationships, it is recommended that you help your children heal the pattern and its underlying belief."

I opened my eyes and saw that Paula was crying.

"So what my spirit is telling me is that it's too late—
I've already ruined my kids!"

"Uh, that's not what I heard," I said cautiously.
"Let me ask your spirit to restate what She meant."

*"Your children are certainly not 'ruined,' as you
say. They have learned this pattern of relating to
loved ones, so they can certainly learn other patterns.
Changing their behavior will occur when you talk
openly about how they are treating one another, and
how trying to be better than the other person means
that you are ultimately hurting someone that you
care about.*

*"It is a common belief that parents should postpone
divorce until their children leave the home in order to
spare them the turmoil of a separation and divorce
proceedings. But it is also important to remember
that children learn about romantic relationships not
by what their parents tell them, but by how their
parents live. So if parents tell their daughter that she
should only date men who respect her, the daughter
will look for evidence of her father treating her mother
with respect. If she observes her father treating her
mother disrespectfully, and the mother accepting the
disrespectful treatment, then she will conclude that
what her parents have told her is unrealistic."*

"Well, then I have definitely ruined my kids
because Monica sees George talk to me in a
disrespectful way all the time! And I tell her that it's
not okay for her dad to talk to me like that—calling
me an idiot and an airhead—but..."

"But you stay," I said, finishing Paula's sentence.

She hung her head and said quietly, "Yeah,
I stay."

I wanted to be encouraging, but I also knew that this was the time for Paula to peel off the covers and look honestly at what was happening. "What I'm hearing your spirit say is that what's even more important than what we tell our kids is what we show them. And so if you tell your daughter that it's not okay to let a man call you an idiot, but you live with a man who calls you that, then you're actually teaching her that the ideal is not possible, and she will have to settle for an unhealthy relationship just like you have."

"Oh! That's horrible," Paula wailed. "But what does a divorce show her? That there's no such thing as happily ever after, and she should just give up on finding a loving husband?"

"I think it can show her that you're not willing to tolerate being treated poorly, and that if a relationship is unhealthy, and the other person isn't willing to help you heal it, then you'll need to leave. Again, we teach our kids healthy boundaries by demonstrating them, not just stating ideas to them." I could feel Paula's spirit trying to connect with me again, so I closed my eyes to focus on hearing Her.

"The process of divorce is not an easy one and should not be taken lightly. But your children are at an age where they are very intrigued by romantic relationships, and they are noticing everything that you and George are modeling for them. Part of your job as a parent is to teach them what a healthy relationship is and is not, and this includes the subject of healthy boundaries around how each person is treated.

"How you allow another person to treat you makes

a statement about what you believe is possible and what treatment you believe that you deserve."

Paula held up her hand in protest. "Whoa! Are You saying that I think that I'm an idiot? Because I certainly do not!"

"No, not that you believe that you're an idiot. But perhaps you believe that you and George will never treat each other kindly because you have each hurt each other too many times in the past. Your guilt over your own hurtful behavior may keep you from insisting on more loving behavior from George."

"Well, yes. I can agree with that," Paula nodded.

"But this idea leaves both of you in a hole that you can never dig out of. You feel resentment towards your spouse who reminds you of all the hurtful behavior that you've done in the past, and in your frustration, you lash out, creating new damage that you'll regret and will be punished for. It is an endless cycle. To stop it will require a conscious effort to walk away from this pattern where you each justify hurting the other one because he/she has hurt you in the past. Now you each allow the other to strike you verbally because on some level you agree that you have 'earned it' by your own harsh statements."

Paula sighed. "God, this sounds miserable. I refuse to live this way any longer! George can't be happy living like this either."

"No, he isn't happy with this lifestyle, but he may not believe that another option exists. It's recommended that you explain to George what you now understand—about the patterns that you and he are living and how they are being duplicated by your children. Inform him that you have decided not

to live this way anymore, and therefore the options as you see them are: 1) for the two of you to get help in transforming how you treat each other, or 2) divorcing."

I felt anxious, and so I broke off my connection with Paula's spirit to interject my own opinion. "Paula, make sure that you really are determined not to live this way anymore. Sometimes people say that, but they really are so afraid of change that, in the end, they'll keep choosing to live miserably rather than venture into the unknown. I don't want you to bring up divorce unless you really are prepared to do it. I've seen so many couples who throw around the 'divorce' word like a threat until neither of them takes it seriously anymore, and in the meantime, the kids have become terrified that any given day could end in divorce. That's just my two cents, having worked with so many couples who have threatened each other with divorce."

Paula smiled a bittersweet smile. "Unfortunately I already know what you're talking about. Whenever George thinks that I've been flirting with another guy, he threatens to divorce me. Never mind the fact that he's had several emotional affairs and one physical one. But no, I hear ya. I don't throw that word around, so he will probably sit up and take notice when I say it calmly and firmly. And I *am* done. I'm done living like this and modeling what a toxic relationships looks like for my kids. I'm tired of my son talking disrespectfully to me and me just letting him because the whole house feels like a war zone, and I don't have the strength to fight with both George and my son."

Paula sat up straighter and took a deep breath.

"But as I sit here talking with you and my spirit, I realize that too much damage is being done by living this way, and that I'm not sparing anyone by avoiding divorce. I look forward to living with more peace and love around me. I hope that this is with George, but if not, then that's okay. And I look forward to modeling what a healthy relationship looks like for both of my kids. I want to be proud of how my son treats his girlfriends and how my daughter insists on healthy relationships. I feel optimistic for the first time in years!"

I told Paula that her enthusiasm would likely waver, but her spirit would be here to guide her through whatever the next steps turned out to be. She booked a follow-up appointment and left looking far more hopeful than she did when she arrived.

Follow-up:

Paula has been moving through a very difficult time. She and her husband decided to divorce, but in the following weeks her husband told her that he did not want all the upheaval that a divorce would bring and asked Paula to remain in the marriage. Paula declined, recognizing that she didn't want to stay married out of a fear of change. This has created increased hostility between them, and Paula is trying to insulate the children from their arguments as much as possible.

In the meantime Paula continues to do her own healing work, getting clearer on how she participated in the disintegration of the relationship and deciding how she wants to move forward in all of her relationships. She is learning to watch for what I call "emotional quicksand"—patterns of thought that pull you down so that you react from a low version of yourself. This is an emotionally trying time for Paula, but she readily admits that there have been compelling moments of learning and empowerment as she works to intentionally create the person she now wishes to be.

Chapter 24

Sharon's Case – Healing Brain Trauma

Because I used to practice law, I think the Universe thinks it's fun to send me clients who are lawyers. My spirit tells me it's because I'm skillful at building a bridge between the way a lawyer is trained to think and my current perspective, but I wonder if it's really because God has a sense of humor.

Last week I saw a new client named Sharon, a lawyer who had a very interesting set of symptoms. She sent me her background information in an email because her speech was slurred and difficult to understand over the phone. Sharon was in a car accident five years ago. Her injuries from the accident appeared similar to those of a stroke victim, although tests revealed that she had not suffered a stroke during the crash. She worked diligently during her rehabilitation and eventually recovered full functionality.

But as a result of the accident, she had seizures two or three times each year. These seizures were triggered by loud noises, and when they occurred, Sharon would fall over and be unable to coordinate her muscles for several minutes. Her speech would be incoherent and would take ten to fifteen minutes to regain normalcy. Doctors could not figure out the mechanism by which these seizures occurred, and since Sharon's life was otherwise "back to normal," she had simply learned to live with them.

At the five-year anniversary of Sharon's car accident, she had three seizures over a five-day period. The third seizure did not follow the same pattern as the others; the symptoms did not abate, but instead remained in full force. Sharon had great difficulty speaking and stuttered so much that it was frequently difficult to understand her. She also had impaired control of the muscles on the right side of her body, and they would spasm sporadically. She might reach for a glass of water and knock it over instead of picking it up.

Sharon reported that her doctors had run the full battery of tests, including a spinal tap, brain scan, etc. No one had come up with any explanation for the symptoms, and the only solution that was offered was to use steroids, which had produced minimal improvement. Sharon had decided to venture outside of the mainstream Western medicine that she felt comfortable with in the hopes of finding new healing options. A coworker had given her my name and explained that I was most definitely outside the scope of mainstream medicine.

When Sharon had called to book her session, I explained to her what I do in a session, and I could feel her skeptical reaction even though she remained silent on the other end of the phone. She asked, "How m-m-many sess-sess-sessions will I need before I s-s-s-see results from your work?"

I opened my mouth to offer my standard response, which is, "There is no set pattern for my type of work because most of what I do is to approach the symptoms from the emotional level. As you shift your perception and understanding, physical symptoms almost always heal. Sometimes this happens in one session, but usually it takes several sessions. Hopefully you'll feel a difference from the first session. If you don't feel any shift, then you'll know that this type of work is not the most effective option for you."

I swear I opened my mouth ready to say those words and instead what came out was, "It will take one session. If I can do it, I'll do it in one session."

As soon as I heard myself saying those words, I froze in horror. Holy sh**! Who makes that kind of crazy promise? Was I insane? Had my brain and mouth just suffered seizures of their own? But I didn't know how to take the words back without sounding pathetic, so I just prayed that if my spirit was the one who prompted such an insane guarantee, She could back it up.

Sharon arrived on time and was dressed casually. I noticed that she was wearing sweats and a t-shirt (no buttons or zippers to try to wrestle with) and slip-on shoes. She tried to reiterate the story that she had (thankfully) sent me via email, but eventually gave up when I reassured her that I had remembered what she had written. I immediately asked Sharon to sit back and relax while I connected to her spirit.

I was nervous about this case, so I'm afraid I was a bit abrupt with her spirit.

"What's going on with this poor woman?" I asked.

"Sharon's brain was damaged in the car accident. While it was healing, her brain had to set up an alternate pathway to connect to her muscles and to resume her normal speech. Once this pathway was constructed, she was able to pursue physical therapy and regain most of her functionality. Once her brain had healed, she returned to using the standard, or normal, pathways, and she was deemed 'fully recovered.'

"Her seizures were indeed triggered by loud noises, but it was not just any loud noise that triggered each seizure. Some noises carried the same pitch, volume, and intensity as the sound of screeching metal that Sharon heard during the car accident. Such noises triggered an emotional response from Sharon, and she would subconsciously be taken back to the time of the accident. Because she was emotionally reverting to an earlier time, it signaled the brain to resume using the alternate pathways that were established during the brain's healing process. During the transition from the 'normal pathways' to the 'alternate pathways,' Sharon would experience her symptoms."

I asked Sharon's spirit to pause so that I could relay all of this information to Sharon. Her response was, "Oh my God! I've been t-t-t-telling people that it f-f-f-f-feels like I have two routes in the b-b-b-brain, and I just can't s-s-s-switch b-b-b-back over to the good one!"

With this validation from Sharon, I resumed my

conversation with her spirit.

"Sharon's symptoms remained with her after her last seizure because I decided that it was time for her to begin the next step on her path. She has spent way too much of her life disconnected from her heart and relying almost exclusively on her mind for wisdom. I have three requests of Sharon. Please tell her that I want her to:

1. *Do what you love,*
2. *Spend time with people that you love to be with, and*
3. *Be happy."*

I interrupted Sharon's spirit, silently chiding Her. "Look, this woman is a high-powered attorney who has just had her career potentially derailed because of these symptoms. I don't think that she's going to want to hear these suggestions. Frankly, they sound like something from the inside of a lame greeting card. If You want her to start a spiritual practice, I think that You should suggest something more profound."

"Please repeat the suggestions to Sharon just as I have laid them out for you," Sharon's spirit gently insisted.

I grumbled to myself (and to Sharon's spirit) and repeated what I had heard. To my utter amazement, Sharon looked at me like I had shared a profound revelation. "I've b-b-b-been getting that m-m-message, or those messages, over and over. Hearing s-s-s-song lyrics that say those th-th-th-things or hearing them f-f-f-from friends and doctors.

That's amazing!"

Okay, once again I've established that the Universe knows a whole lot more than I do. I reconnected to Sharon's spirit.

"To heal Sharon's symptoms, you will need to use energy to shut down the alternative pathways in the brain. I will show you where they are as you stream healing energy into her head; just follow My directions. There will be some mild discomfort for Sharon, so let her know that before you begin."

I relayed this to Sharon, and she eagerly got up on the treatment table, much more confident than I was in that moment. I followed the line that Sharon's spirit drew for me, placing energy with the intent to shut down the alternate pathway in her brain. Twenty-five minutes later, I finished and asked Sharon to sit up and tell me how she felt.

"I feel a bit lightheaded, but otherwise fine. Hey! No stuttering! Can you hand me a pencil, and let me try to grab it with my right hand?"

I handed Sharon a pencil, and to the amazement of both of us, she reached out and grasped it with ease. We both looked at each other in disbelief—I think I may have had more shock on my face than she did. When she stood up, she wobbled and my heart sank.

"Don't worry—just give her some food," my spirit quickly urged.

I went downstairs and grabbed some tuna fish out of the fridge, some crackers, and a glass of water. I felt like a mother bird as I put small bites of tuna on crackers and fed them to Sharon for a few minutes, and then she insisted on trying to walk again. I held my breath and exhaled with relief as she got off the table and smoothly walked around the room.

"Okay, now try to talk," I suggested. Sharon spoke easily with no stutter or hesitation. We both sat looking at each other with huge grins on our faces. Then, suddenly, Sharon's face looked apprehensive. I raised my eyebrows questioningly.

"I think I'm afraid to walk out of this treatment room," she said, "for fear that everything will revert back once I leave." I closed my eyes and connected to her spirit to hear Her guidance.

"It's important that Sharon understand that her symptoms are gone, and they are not meant to return. In order to recreate these symptoms, Sharon would have to work at it for quite some time. If each time Sharon hears a loud noise, she recoils, waiting for her symptoms to return, she may eventually create another alternative pathway in her brain. It will not be the same one that you have just used energy to collapse—that one is permanently gone. But over time, she could create a new one with her expectations, which can direct the brain. So when she leaves here today, Sharon is advised to celebrate her recovery and banish all fears of a recurrence of her symptoms."

"Okay, done!" Sharon agreed enthusiastically. As she left my house, she practically skipped up the driveway to her car. As she climbed into her car, I heard her talking to her boyfriend on her cell phone.

"No, I'm all better. I swear! Yes, just like that. Well, I can't really explain it, she just...did some stuff with energy, and...now I'm back! Oh, and there's a message too, sort of a teaching that I'm supposed to take away from all of this today. I don't totally understand it, but I'll tell you more when I get home."

I walked back into my house smiling and shaking my head too.

Follow-up:

A few days later I called Sharon, and she reported that she was still symptom-free. I asked her to check in with me via email in another week, perhaps because I was still incredulous that her treatment had worked so thoroughly. Two weeks later Sharon emailed to verify that she was "all good." Later that day as I sat in meditation, my spirit commented on Sharon's session.

"I see that you are still in amazement over the help that you were able to give to Sharon. Why is that?"

I didn't have to think about my answer. "Because I've worked on so many people, and that kind of dramatic, permanent recovery is rare! I wish that I saw immediate healings like that every day in my practice, but the truth is that they hardly ever happen that way. And since I can't explain why some people experience these miraculous sessions and others take months to heal, it makes me uncomfortable."

My spirit's answer came accompanied by very reassuring energy. *"I know that when you do not understand something, it makes you uncomfortable, so I will try to offer insight.*

"Your clients will always receive the exact healing that they need in that moment to help them along on their path. Every client has an ego, and the ego wishes for a complete end to all physical suffering

and emotional discomfort. Because you also have an ego, you tend to want what the client's ego wants. This reassures the client, as you appear to be 'on her team,' but in truth, you would be better served to see yourself as working for the client's spirit."

I felt confused, which made my energy drop, which broke off my connection with my spirit. I took a deep breath, cleared my mind, and raised my energy up and reconnected with Her. "Why is it better to see myself as working for a client's spirit?" I asked. "It's the client's ego that runs things, right? Her ego makes the decision to book a session with me and writes the check at the end of the session. Isn't that really who I'm working for?"

"While it's true that the client's ego makes the decision to book a session with you, it's the client's spirit that helps to create the symptoms and maintain them in the body. Since persistent physical symptoms frequently contain a message from the spirit, it is the spirit that determines when it's time to release the symptom and allow healing to occur. Most of your clients, and you yourself, view an improvement in physical symptoms as an indication that you are on the right track. Thus physical improvements serve as a sort of barometer, letting you and your clients know that they are shifting into a more balanced way of living."

"Okay, but then why do some clients get these spontaneous healings that look miraculous?" I queried.

"Because in some cases, the client's spirit determines that the best way to awaken the client to the truths laid before her is to have a dramatic healing

occur. So you share the spirit's advice through your channeling, and then the spirit supports the body's release of the corresponding physical symptoms. This tends to make a very strong impact on the client's ego, as you witnessed the day of Sharon's session with you. Both you and Sharon took very seriously what her spirit had to say, especially after witnessing her dramatic recovery. Sharon is very analytical and has been trying many different healing modalities in an attempt to return to her job. If her symptoms had just improved slightly, it might have been easy for her to attribute her improved condition to other factors and to make light of the messages that you channeled for her. Do you think that she will forget those messages now?"

"No, definitely not!" I agreed. "So does this mean that how much a person heals has nothing to do with me, it's just whatever her spirit decides once the client gets here?" I was beginning to feel a bit like a gas pump, delivering healing energy like some sort of fuel.

"No, you are most definitely a factor. In fact the precise timing of Sharon's session with you had more to do with your journey than with hers. Do you remember how you were feeling on the day before her session? You were filled with doubts, wondering if you were really hearing Me and other spirits. You were in need of healing too—spiritual healing. And it was time for Sharon to begin her own spiritual journey. So her spirit and I decided that we would bring the two of you together to experience a 'miracle' of sorts."

"That is humbling, I must say. And daunting.

How do I know how much healing to expect each client to have? If I tell the client that the reason she didn't experience much physical healing is because her spirit didn't allow that, it sounds like I'm making an excuse for why my energy healing treatment didn't work."

"Yes, it may sound like an excuse to some of your clients. But I don't advise you to avoid the truth simply because some people won't approve of it or believe it."

"Easy for You to say!" I said a bit too defensively.

"Yes, it is." My spirit answered gently. *"And this is why I recommend that you view yourself as working for each client's spirit more than her ego. Because you will never be able to make each client's ego happy since you cannot always deliver exactly the result that the ego seeks. But if you are dedicated to connecting to each client's spirit and communicating what is offered, then you will feel in harmony with the Universe and be fulfilling your goal to be of service.*

"Which leads me to an important piece of advice that I would like to offer you: If you always want what the Universe wants, you will always be happy."

"Well that makes sense, I guess, since the Universe, or God, always gets Its way because It is vast and all-powerful. So it's like aligning yourself with the side that's guaranteed to win."

I could feel my spirit smiling. *"I don't recommend that you hold the intention for your desires to match the Universe's desires so that you always win, but so that you minimize your own suffering. This decision to align your intentions with the Universe's intentions should be based on the understanding that if you knew all of the details—of the past, present, and future—that you would choose for things to go exactly as they are unfolding."*

"Wait! You are saying that I would choose for the client I saw last week to have been in that terrible car accident that she is still recovering from (two more surgeries at least), and that I would choose for the client I saw yesterday to have been molested as a child?! I'm having trouble believing that I would support those decisions."

My spirit was ready with Her answer. *"But that is because you don't realize that the client who is recovering from the car accident has learned so much about asking for help and letting others assist her without feeling guilty. This was a teaching that her spirit asked for and the Universe granted it—not to promote suffering, but to assist the spirit in its efforts to help the ego evolve.*

"And the client who was molested as a child chose that painful past so that she would have a reason to leave her family home at 16 and never look back. In her three lifetimes prior to this one, she dedicated herself to her family to such a degree that she never pursued her own dreams. She has a hard time making boundaries once she is here in physical form, and so by choosing an abusive family situation, she created for herself a motivation to leave and be able to pursue her own dreams. It does also mean that she has wounds from her past that she needs to heal, as do all humans, but in the end, her spirit is content with her choice because it accomplished the desired goal.

"Since you cannot know the entire story behind

every event that occurs, you will experience endless frustration if you judge the events rather than honoring the choices of each spirit. But if you assume that each occurrence in the Universe is intentional and is helping each spirit accomplish a goal, then you will make fewer mistakes than you would if you were to chase after the goals of each client's ego, and you will experience less frustration."

I had to sit for awhile to absorb what my spirit shared. I realized how often in my conversations with Her I ended up in this place, realizing how little we all understand about why things happen in the ways that they do, and the assumptions that we each make. The Universe is so complex and feels like a gigantic play that is perfectly choreographed. From my seat at the edge of the stage, I see only a fraction of what is occurring. But my spirit has a perspective that is more like an aerial view, and She comprehends and appreciates the interweaving of the different events and the perfect timing of each. And yet still I dispute the way that things unfold! Telling my spirit how I think things should be unfolding and campaigning for my desired results. Talk about wasted energy! I suppose that's the lawyer side of my brain that won't give up once I've formed an opinion about the way things should be. Another bad ego habit that I need to eliminate.

Chapter 25

Mark & Lauren's Case – Romance Reality

My next appointment was Mark, the husband of one of my long-time clients Lauren. Mark had suffered from back pain for many years, and after I used energy to adjust Lauren's hips and back, he noticed how much better she felt, and he called for a session. Mark's back pain was in a different location than his wife's pain. Lauren's was in her lower-back, but Mark's discomfort was centered in the middle of his back, directly behind his stomach. Mark was in good shape and exercised regularly, but still had back pain most of the time. Tests had verified that there was no structural damage to his back, and so Mark's doctors had recommended that he treat his back pain with over-the-counter anti-inflammatory medication such as Ibuprofen. But Mark was not getting much relief from the anti-inflammatory medications and was hesitant to ask his doctor for stronger drugs because of their potential side effects.

Lauren and Mark arrived together, since they

planned to go out to lunch after Mark's session. Mark was in his early 40s, attractive, and appeared to be in good shape. Lauren said goodbye and prepared to go to a local coffee shop for the hour that Mark was in session. To my surprise, I heard myself saying, "Wait, I want to ask Mark's spirit about you staying." Ordinarily I prefer to see each client alone for the first session, but I had a strong feeling that Lauren was supposed to be a part of Mark's session. Sure enough, when I connected to Mark's spirit, I heard that it would be helpful if Lauren participated in Mark's session.

As the session began and I asked Mark some introductory questions, I could tell by observing his energy that he was a fairly confident man who enjoyed his work as a corporate analyst. He liked the problem-solving aspect of his work, and he enjoyed the people that he worked with. He was very successful financially and had a natural charisma. Mark and Lauren had been married for ten years and had two healthy children, aged 6 and 8. "Life is great," he said more than once, but his energy didn't match his wording, and I wondered if he was trying to convince himself or me. So I looked over to Lauren and asked her, "*Is* your life great?"

"Sure," she answered hesitatingly, "but things could always be better, right?"

"In what way?" I asked.

"Well...you know... You could always want more money...or more...passion...," and her voice trailed off. I glanced over at Mark, who looked deflated compared to how he had looked just moments ago. Still watching Mark out of the corner of my eye, I asked Lauren if there had been a lot of passion in the beginning of their relationship.

"Oh yes! We were young and in love and had a great time. But now we've been together for a long time, and I guess you just trade comfort and stability for passion, right?"

I knew that I was circling in on something important, but rather than spend time asking questions to try to root it out, I went straight to the source—Mark's spirit.

As soon as I connected to Mark's spirit, He suggested that I ask Lauren about her favorite movies. When I did, Mark groaned and said, "I can answer that one! She has three favorites: *The Notebook* and the two *Twilight* movies. She can't get enough of those first-love, intense romance movies." As Mark spoke, I could see the energy in his middle back area, and it was getting black and dark red with the frustration that he was feeling.

Now I was beginning to understand the emotional issues behind Mark's back pain. His pain was located in an area of the body where we register our impressions of ourselves, how we see ourselves, and how we think that other people perceive us. Mark's spirit helped me feel that while Mark's employer was pleased with his performance, his wife was not. Lauren had sent her youngest child off to school earlier in the year and was beginning to feel unfulfilled. She yearned to feel more valuable in her life and more purposeful. Watching the first-love movies that she enjoyed helped her remember a time in her life when she felt vibrant and passionate. The problem was that they also represented a time and situation that she could not recreate in her current life, and so she was left feeling unfulfilled and empty.

As a man who took pleasure in being a problem-solver, Mark was being presented with a problem that he couldn't solve in his marriage. He couldn't go back in time and recreate the original passion that he and his wife had during the first year of their relationship, for many reasons. Mark's spirit spoke to both Lauren and Mark.

"It's important to realize that when you watch movies like Twilight and The Notebook, you step so far out of your current reality that you create suffering for yourself. You do this by wishing that your current adult life matched the imaginary life of an 18 year old in love for the first time. When you're young and fall in love for the first time, you typically have very few responsibilities other than school or a part-time job. You don't have many financial responsibilities since you don't own a home, you don't have kids to take care of, and you don't have huge debts to pay off. You don't have to think about anyone—or anything— other than the fulfillment of your immediate desires, which are completely centered on another person. You have no experience in putting limitations around such passion and infatuation and neither does the other person. So you're off and running, thinking about this person obsessively, and believing that this behavior means that you're truly in love.

"Why can't you ever capture this type of passion again? Well, one reason is that hopefully your life has become fuller and more complex than when you were 18. You probably have mortgages, kids, pets,

and a career that demand some of your focus and attention. This narrows down the amount of intense energy that you can send to one person, as your time and energy are divided amongst several things that you feel strongly about.

"But even more restrictive on that flow of heart energy coming out of you is your life experience. When you're in love for the first time, you've watched movies and read books that teach you that your first love usually doesn't last. But because you've never been in love before, you don't have any way of comparing what you feel to what others have felt, and you are sure that what you feel is different. No one has felt this intensity before, this much love, this much passion. Surely you and your love will be the exception to the rule, the one in a million couple that meets, falls in love, and remains in love forever."

Lauren laughed. "Oh boy—do I remember feeling like that with my first love!"

"Once that relationship ends, so does your naïveté. Now you know—experientially as well as theoretically—that most relationships end at some point. And from then on, you love less fully. You don't risk all of your heart because then there is more of you out there, vulnerable to getting hurt. You protect yourself more by risking less. And as you get older, you try to protect your heart more and more. You're more guarded, more suspicious, and more ready to take a simple comment the wrong way. You reveal less of yourself and judge the other person more readily, which leads to offering less love and more criticism. Sex may become more mechanical as the emotional energy is withheld until your lover

passes some unknown test. And you arrive in that place where relationships look much better on the big screen or in a book than they do in your life. And the resentment builds. You miss the feeling of being loved unconditionally, not realizing that you yourself are loving your partner with many conditions."

I stopped channeling for a moment and opened my eyes. Mark looked relieved, and Lauren looked sad. I raised my eyebrows questioningly at her, and she asked, "So does this mean that I should give up on feeling that love?"

I knew better than to try and answer that one myself, so I closed my eyes and reconnected to Mark's spirit.

"What you're missing—truly missing in your life— is the feeling of intense love and of very little judgment from your partner. These feelings are available to you even though you are no longer experiencing your first love. The heart yearns for fewer restrictions on the sending and receiving of love. You can move in this direction and find enormous happiness together.

"What are no longer available to you are the feelings that stemmed from your ego when you were a teenager. The heart yearns to feel loved, while the ego yearns to feel special, better than everyone else. Movies that show someone loving a person so much that he jeopardizes his own health or safety seem appealing because our ego wants to feel so special that someone can love us beyond all reason, even beyond his instinct for safety. But as an adult, if someone loved you in this way, you would likely think of him as unbalanced, or possibly even a stalker. You would wonder why he wasn't more focused on

his career or spending time with his children. The qualities that make Mark a good man and a good husband in your eyes make him a lousy romantic lead in a teen romance movie."

"I'm embarrassed," Lauren confessed. "I see how what I was looking for is not even possible in my current life. I don't want to give up our kids and your great job, and the life that we've created. I think that what I was looking for was to feel special again, like when we first met and it seemed like your whole world revolved around me. I'm sorry!"

Lauren's spirit spoke then: *"Lauren, it's wonderful to want more passion in your life, but you shouldn't have to give up anything that you've accomplished in your life in order to get it.*"

Then I heard from both Mark and Lauren's spirits. They suggested that Mark and Lauren have a date night once a month. Of course they could go out every week if they liked, but once a month there was to be a special date night. They would take turns being responsible for the entire evening, from where they went, to hiring the babysitter, to choosing the clothing that the other person wore. I had heard this suggestion from the spirit world before, and it had produced great results for other couples that I had worked with, including Ann and Tom.

"Wait!" Lauren sounded nervous. "Mark gets to choose the clothes that I will wear? What if he chooses something skimpy that I don't feel comfortable in?!"

Mark was already getting into the spirit of the idea. "Hey, if it's in your closet then you bought it, so it must be fair game!" he teased. When she looked anxious, he laughed and added, "I'm a pretty decent dresser, don't you think? I know what's appropriate to wear to different venues."

Lauren smiled at him. "Yeah, you're very stylish. Okay, I *do* trust you to pick out something for me to wear. This could be fun!"

Mark's spirit continued. *"Part of the problem here is predictability. Humans crave it, but then when they achieve the stability of a solid relationship, they miss the sense of adventure that comes from not knowing what's ahead. If you can interject spontaneity into a stable relationship, then you can have the best of both worlds. Part of Lauren's attraction to the relationships in those movies is the tension of the unknown future. Yet if she was in such a place of uncertainty herself, it is very unlikely that she would enjoy it as much."*

"Oh, I'm sure that's true!" Lauren agreed, grinning. "And I don't know where Mark will take me for our first 'date night,' but I can live with that level of uncertainty."

Because Mark now had a problem that he could solve—planning a romantic night out for himself and his wife—the energy in his middle back had turned from a mixture of black and red to a shade of yellow that corresponds to happiness. At that point I could give Mark an energy treatment, confident that the healing energy would be used by his body to soothe and repair the inflamed tissue.

Six weeks later I saw Lauren for a session. She gushed about how she and Mark were communicating better and were focusing on not criticizing each other.

"We hadn't even realized how we had each built up this list of grudges, dumb little faults that we were keeping track of as evidence of how the other person wasn't a good enough spouse. Now we're really trying to appreciate how hard we both work to keep the marriage—and our family—happy. Sometimes that involves surprises and spontaneity, and sometimes it's a comforting cup of coffee together Sunday morning in bed with the kids. Mark's back is fine—now that I've gotten off it!" she laughed.

I love working with couples. Not every couple moves through their problems as quickly as Mark and Lauren, but hearing from both spirits in a session gives such a great perspective that resolutions tend to come very quickly. And at times, I feel like a lucky fly on the wall, getting all this great relationship advice for free!

Follow-up:

While Mark and Lauren have experienced great healing in their own relationship, they both continue to see me—together and separately—for help with issues involving kids, friends, and family members. They truly live as a conscious family, noticing when issues feel heavy and stuck and coming in for a session to ask the spirit world for guidance.

Chapter 26

My Statute of Limitations

Working with Mark and Lauren the other day made me think about one of the important policies that I utilize in all my relationships.

My family has its share of wackiness, just like yours, but one of the things that I'm very grateful for is that in my family, your past mistakes are almost never thrown in your face. This was never a spoken rule, it just didn't happen. My mom was adamant about talking things through until each person had clarity about what was bothering her and what was bothering the other person too. There was such a sense of completion after these conversations that we generally didn't feel the need to bring the incident up again.

This was something that I took for granted, assuming that other families operated this way. When my friends in college and law school began complaining about arguments that they'd had with friends or lovers months or years ago, I was confused. "Didn't you resolve that back when it happened?" I would ask. And they would look at me like I was slow witted. And when friends or boyfriends tried to bring up an old infraction that I had committed in the past, I refused to play. This has led me to a rule which I now refer to as my "statute of limitations."

My statute of limitations goes something like this: If there is any wrong that you feel I have done to you, please let me know. I truly care about the people in my life, and I want to heal any wound that I've created. But I ask that you notify me of any mistake that I've made within a short period of time. I prefer immediately, but I understand that sometimes we each have to sit with something before we're able to articulate what is upsetting us. Once you bring this event or misunderstanding to my attention, I promise to sit down and talk about it until we're both clear about what happened and why. Usually within that conversation, my motivation will become clear, and so will yours, and we'll realize that even though we may have hurt each other's feelings, that was never our intent, and we will feel resolved.

The only time I will bring up a past behavior that we've already discussed is when I am trying to assess if there is a pattern that needs to be addressed, and I invite you to do the same. There may be times where we have to agree to disagree, and if so, then we'll determine if our relationship can continue in a healthy way with this between us. If we decide that it can, then we will each make an effort to let it go and commit to not using it as a club to beat the other person up with. In this way, our relationship will always be about who each of us is today, not who we were last month or last year, and the mistakes we made as that person.

This is my "golden rule" for all of my relationships, and I've ended friendships and romantic relationships because the other person couldn't follow this plan and just couldn't resist bringing up past misunderstandings as evidence that I wasn't caring enough, or thoughtful enough, or that I was just wrong. I can't see why anyone would want to live with this feeling that there's an anvil hanging over her head, waiting to drop whenever the other person feels like reminding her of some past mistake. That just doesn't feel loving to me, and I don't want to do that to anyone or have it done to me.

Many couples that I've worked with have adopted this rule for themselves and have always raved about how it improved their relationships. This policy focuses on the underlying intentions of each person more than the mistakes made. When you're allowed to be free from your past lapses in judgment, you'll walk around with less guilt and shame, and that's always a good thing!

If you were raised in a family that routinely used your past mistakes against you, then this may be a hard habit to break. I've worked with several women who loved the idea of this statute of limitations on past injuries, but were unable to employ it in their relationships, particularly their marriages. In moments of feeling hurt, each woman felt that she couldn't convince her husband of how hurtful he had been. So to bolster her argument of how insensitive and hurtful he was, she would throw in old mistakes, piling them on top of his current error, to prove to him that he was the problem in the relationship.

Most people have done this—trotting out lists of past mistakes the other person has made—as if we're mounting a legal case, determined to prove that we're the better person. My friend Sandy refers to this as building an evidence pile. But if you succeed, and convince him to feel ashamed of himself, then what are you left with? In my opinion, you've won the battle but lost something infinitely more precious— an emotionally safe, loving relationship. I want a man who feels strong and equal to me. And if I beat him down to the ground in order to prove to him that I'm better or right on an issue, then I run the risk of making him feel small and having that feeling stick beyond the end of that argument.

This isn't to say that I'm the ideal woman to be in a relationship with—I can give you a few names of men who would declare that dating me was not always easy. When I was younger, I was passionate and intense in every direction. So if I was in an argument, I was in it to win, and my competitive nature squashed the confidence of more than one young man. Afterwards I would wonder why we never recovered the emotional safety and passion that existed before I'd made him feel wrong/foolish/ naïve/etc. But I've learned over the years that winning isn't everything, and if the other person walks away feeling small, then I've lost too. So while I may not look as youthful as I did at 25, I know that I'm a much softer, wiser person than I was then, and most days I see this as a fair trade-off, a few wrinkles in exchange for compassion and wisdom.

Chapter 27

Lecturing in the Corporate World

I'm so grateful that my career gives me the opportunity to use my skills in so many different ways. This afternoon I was hired to give a lecture to a group of seventy-five people at a toy company in Los Angeles. Typically I'm brought in to help corporate employees understand and reduce their stress levels. Today was a bit different because the employees were allowed to bring their family members along. I did my "Understanding Stress" lecture, in which I describe my understanding of physical symptoms as a series of messages. I compare the human body to a smart phone, with each person's spirit leaving text messages there in the form of symptoms.

This is very different from the paradigm I was raised with, which seems to hold that the body is like a machine. Like a machine, parts of our bodies will eventually wear out or break down, and these parts will need to be fixed or replaced. In this model, we only need to tune in to our body when things go awry, and then we go to the doctor for assistance in fixing or suppressing the uncomfortable symptoms.

I began the lecture with some questions: "What if your spirit was talking to you every day about how you internalize stress? What if He was giving you guidance about the issues you were facing—what would that look like?

A few people offered humorous guesses, and after the chuckles, everyone looked at me expectantly, so I continued.

"What I've learned from the spirit world is that our spirits are communicating with us constantly— through feelings. But because we've not been trained to pay much attention to how we feel (in fact we've been taught to pay more attention to how other people seem to feel *about us*), these feelings are usually ignored or suppressed. When this happens, our spirits try again. They send us messages in a form that is harder for us to ignore—physical symptoms. You know that frequent stomachache, or headache, or tight neck? Those symptoms can just be thought of as 'stress,' or they can be further understood as messages, signals from your spirit about how your life is out of balance. Tonight I'm going to ask you to consider relating to your body and its symptoms differently."

I then reviewed some common symptoms and the types of emotional stress that usually correspond to them. After that brief talk on how I see the body as a sort of road map giving us clues about the areas of our life that need some attention, I offered to answer questions and do "mini-readings" on members of the audience.

The first hand up belonged to a woman (I don't

think I've ever had a man ask the first question). She said, "My name is Betty. I clench my teeth so badly—I think I have since I was young—that my jaw is always sore and throbbing. Do you think that there is a message or an emotional issue behind this?"

As soon as Betty stopped talking, her spirit said, *"She is very afraid to speak her truth. There were terrible repercussions to speaking her truth as a child, and she still does not feel safe to speak up and be heard."*

I relayed this message to Betty, who nodded her head vigorously and said, "There's no point in speaking up now; my husband never hears me, and he usually just gets mad and yells."

As I looked at Betty and focused on just seeing her energy, I saw two red bands of taut muscle on either side of her neck. They looked tight and angry, and they connected up to the back of her jaw. I described what I saw, and Betty smiled, "Well, that would explain why my neck is always stiff too."

Betty's spirit recommended that she begin journaling, a common recommendation for people who have stopped speaking their truth, either because they think no one will hear them or because there will be too high a price to pay for speaking out. Because Betty was concerned that her husband would read it and become angry, Betty's spirit suggested that she journal on her computer. Then as she finished, she could erase the entire entry, and there would be no chance of there being a punishment from her husband reading it and disagreeing with her. When Betty said, "I don't know if I could figure out what to write...," her spirit spoke again.

"When people learn to keep quiet in order to keep the peace and avoid trouble, they do so by suppressing their true feelings and this causes emotional discomfort. To minimize this discomfort, most people suppress the feelings and then try to ignore them completely, in the hopes that the discomfort will go away. This weakens the connection between the person and her spirit, as your spirit communicates with you through feelings. Once you get into the habit of ignoring your feelings, it can be difficult to access them quickly when you are curious about how you really feel about issues.

"But as soon as you hold the intention to reconnect with your spirit, and with your true feelings, you will begin feeling them again. Be patient with yourself as you journal. Start by asking yourself the question: What are some feelings that I had today? You will be pleasantly surprised at how quickly you can reconnect with your heart's voice."

Betty thanked me and nudged the young lady sitting next to her, pushing her to raise her hand. The young lady was her daughter, Carole. Carole said, "I've been diagnosed with rheumatoid arthritis, and I'm only 24 years old! I've had pains that floated around in my body for years, and now I just feel sore all the time. What does my spirit have to say about that?"

Carole's spirit spoke softly, and Her energy felt tender. *"Carole's immune system is responding to a statement that she makes frequently, which is, 'The world is so unfair!' As she has watched her parents' relationship, Carole has concluded that the good guys—like her mother—get ignored and taken for granted, while the bullies get their way. Because she doesn't want to see herself as a bully, she has decided to be more like her mother. But this seems like she's volunteering to be a powerless victim, and that notion makes her frustrated. She feels betrayed by the Universe and what she perceives as a lack of good choices available to her."*

I stopped channeling and opened my eyes to see Carole crying silently in the front row. Another audience member brought her a tissue, and she regained her composure enough to say, "Everything that She says is true. I do see the world that way. Why should my dad get his way all the time? And my boss gets his way, just because he yells and humiliates people, and then gets away with it because he acts nice to the owner of the company."

I had a sense of the lesson that needed to be offered to Carole, but no idea how to say it quickly enough for a short answer in front of an audience. Luckily I could ask Carole's spirit who said, *"There are many different paradigms in the world, and they can all be true simultaneously. Note that a stockbroker living in New York may care very much about how the yen is currently valued compared to the dollar. But the farmer in Kansas is not particularly affected by the yen, and so he is much more concerned with the predicted rainfall that week. The stockbroker is not concerned with the weekly rainfall in Kansas. Whose reality is the most valid, or the most accurate?"*

Carole seemed hesitant. "I guess they both are."

"Exactly. And there are hundreds of thousands

of other perspectives—each equally valid—that place importance on different items. And each person's perspective may include different definitions of power, victims, bullies, and being responsible. If you don't feel happy and empowered in the paradigm in which you were raised, then your personal journey will involve looking for a better paradigm.

"Choose to live in a belief system that makes you feel optimistic, inspired, kindhearted, and empowered. If your beliefs about the world do not make you feel these qualities, keep searching. Look for evidence of other paradigms that are inspiring and spend time around those people. Ask them about their beliefs on relationships, love, self honoring, and generosity. Just as you can choose who you spend time with once you are an adult, you can also choose what you believe. You are not stuck living the same life that your parents live. But to break free of their patterns, you must choose to live a different set of beliefs than theirs."

Carole thanked me and smiled at her mother. "Thanks for telling me to speak up and ask my questions." Her mother hugged her, and I looked around the room for the next person with a question. I noticed a man in the back holding his hand up tentatively. He looked to be in his mid-50s, with salt-and-pepper hair. He spoke quietly, and his energy was calm and confident.

"My name is Bob, and I'm a retired engineer. I admit that I came here to please my wife, who's sitting next to me."

At this point, several other men in the audience chuckled and gave nods of agreement and—if they thought their wives weren't noticing—furtive glances of solidarity.

"But I have to admit, I'm intrigued by what you've said, and by how accurately you've been able to assess these other folks. So I wanted to ask you about my bad back. What can you tell me about it?"

People often ask me if I walk around seeing people as a collection of symptoms. The answer is no. As I mentioned previously, looking at people energetically is like switching to a different channel in my brain. It's like walking into a fancy restaurant and noticing the pretty tables. Then someone points out to you the strangely attired wait staff, and you switch your focus to observe the people instead of the surroundings. Once someone asks me about a physical symptom, their energy field opens up, and their spirit seems to "point out" what I need to pay attention to. So I may see an interesting pattern of energy that relays information to me, or a visual provided by the person's spirit, or I may hear words provided by my own spirit.

So with Bob's permission, I looked through his body to see his spine and the surrounding area. He appeared to have two discs that were inflamed, both of which seemed worn or flattened on the left side and bulging or inflamed on the right side. The right side of his lower-back area held red energy, with dark charcoal-colored bands running through it. I knew that that color of gray mixed with red usually corresponded to feelings of intense resentment.

I relayed all of this to Bob, who looked rather stunned. His wife nodded and smiled, seeming to enjoy the fact that I had accurately described her husband.

Bob spoke slowly. "So...what does that mean?"

"It can mean several things. The right side of our body generally represents our future, and the left side represents the past. So if your symptoms are focused primarily on the left side of your body, it tells me that you may have unhealed portions of your past that are eating up a lot of your energy and attention. And if, as in your case, you have symptoms that are primarily on the right side of your body—"

"Yes, all my pain is on the right side, and sometimes I get sciatic pain on the right side too!" Bob interrupted enthusiastically.

"Okay," I continued, "If the symptoms tend to focus on the right side, then it usually indicates that you have fears about your future that are consuming a lot of your time and energy. The area of your lower-back is an area where we tend to store stress related to power. So when we feel disempowered, this area can become symptomatic. Can you think of how you're feeling disempowered in your life now, some way that has you worried about moving into the future? I sense that this is related to your job."

"Boy, is it ever!" Bob exclaimed. "My company was sold, and the two men that bought it know nothing about our industry but thought that they would learn along the way. Ha! What they're doing is destroying twenty-five years of great customer relationships. And because I'm the VP of sales, I'm putting out the fires every day."

I didn't have time for a long conversation with Bob about how to feel more empowered, so I got his permission to speak to his spirit for some concise advice.

Bob's spirit spoke, and I repeated what I heard: *"Bob's upset for two reasons. The first is the sharp learning curve that his new bosses are going through, and that is causing some ruffled feathers. But the second is that he is very concerned that his retirement plans will now need to be pushed back, and he will have to work for longer than he had intended."*

I opened my eyes and asked Bob if that information felt accurate. "Well, yes. That's true, but it's really the first reason that I think my back is killing me."

Bob's spirit disagreed. *"Bob feels that he is being selfish and not a team player when he focuses on how the sale of the business may impact his retirement. For this reason, he doesn't like to acknowledge this worry, but it's there nonetheless. And because he suppresses this worry, it causes his reactions to be exaggerated when he's dealing with customers. Whenever we suppress an emotion, it doesn't just go away. It distorts and comes out in a different way."*

Bob's shoulders drooped, and he looked a bit defeated. "Yeah, I guess it *is* on my mind a lot. This company was like a family, and we were a great team. But when the owner sold, several of the key people left. I don't want to desert the guys that are still there, but I also don't want to keep working for years until things are smooth with the new owners."

Bob's spirit was speaking with a vibration that felt comforting. *"When the owner sold and key people left, you took on a responsibility that was not yours—that of keeping everyone's morale up and the company standards unblemished. Neither of*

these duties was given to you, and you are weighing
yourself down with a load that is not yours to carry.
Retire as you had planned. The company is moving
in the right direction, and when you leave, others
will get a chance to step in and fill your shoes, and
this will be important growth for those individuals."

This may sound crazy, but I swear I watched his
back muscles unclench as those words came out of
my mouth. He sighed audibly, and all the colors in
his energy field shifted to a shade of pale pink that
corresponds to contentment. He thanked me, and
his wife looked like she wanted to kiss me. Luckily
she kissed her husband instead.

I was just wrapping up the presentation when
a woman in the audience called out, "Why do you
think I have such low energy?" I looked at her
and saw that her energy was very scattered—her
energy field looked like a starburst. It would have
been pretty except that I knew it meant that she
was probably *feeling* scattered as well—not such a
pretty feeling. I described what I saw and asked her
if she felt pulled in many different directions lately.

"You bet!" she said and proceeded to list off a
litany of responsibilities, including getting kids to
music lessons and sporting practices, running her
household, working part-time, and supporting her
husband as he ran his own business. She concluded
with, "But that's life, right?"

I asked her if she bumped into things often and
if she lost items frequently. "Yes and yes!" she said.
"How did you know that?"

"Because when your energy is that scattered,
your focus is too. And you can only focus on so

many items at once. I heard your long list of duties for each day, but you do not have to do all of them simultaneously. If you can work with your mind and train it to focus more on the present moment and what you have to do right now, then you won't feel so scattered, and you will have better focus. For instance, you have been sitting in this room for some time now, but I know that a good deal of your focus is still on those other chores that you did today because all of your energy is still scattered instead of gathered in the center of you. Take a moment and focus on your breathing. I'm not talking about having to close your eyes and meditate—just notice the air going in and out of your lungs for three breaths. We will all do it too."

Some people closed their eyes, and others looked around self-consciously. But as each person noticed their breathing, it became deeper and slower. Thirty seconds later I looked at the woman with the scattered energy and saw that her energy now resembled a soft cloud around her body. Much better! I relayed this to her and watched her smile.

"It's amazing, but I actually feel better, just from that quick exercise!" she exclaimed.

I spoke for a moment about other techniques to gather and focus one's energy, and then ended the presentation with a short guided meditation. As I drove home, I reflected on how different my life is now compared to how I thought it would look when I graduated from law school.

Chapter 28

Justin's Relationship Lessons

I'm frequently asked what my boys think of my job. My answer: It depends what year you're referring to. During middle school, those three challenging years where every boy is trying to fit in and look cool, my boys asked me to refrain from mentioning my career in front of their friends. When the boys got into high school, having a mom who was an intuitive became "cool" because most girls were intrigued by it. And now that my boys are dating, my intuitive abilities have been useful to them in helping them navigate their relationships.

I feel blessed that my boys and I are close and that they feel comfortable discussing their friendships and romantic relationships with me. They're eager to learn about why people act the way that they do. I think they realize that the more you understand about human nature, the less you take things personally that are not really about you. A case in point is a relationship that Justin had last year with a girl named Madison.

Madison is a very pretty girl who is bright and bubbly, and Justin's friends thought that he and Madison made a perfect couple because they were both confident and outgoing. The first two weeks of their relationship went smoothly, but during the third week, I noticed that Justin was increasingly short-tempered at home. By the fourth week, his irritability had increased and prompted his older brother, Joey, to point out, not so delicately, that he was not fun to be around. At this point Justin came upstairs and sat on the edge of my bed while I was making it (not particularly helpful to that process, but a sign that he wanted to talk about something personal).

He looked a bit deflated as he said, "Mom, I think I'm going to break up with Madison."

I've learned that Justin talks more freely if I ask minimal questions at first, so I just raised my eyebrows and said, "Oh?"

"Yeah, well, I'm not enjoying this. She's...different than she was before. Which makes no sense! Her whole personality has changed in just one month!"

I said it was unlikely that her personality had changed significantly in one month, and more likely that she and Justin had different ideas of what a relationship should be like. Once they went from flirtatious friends to romantic partners, she probably had different expectations of him.

"Yeah, before we were a couple, she was in our group of friends. We all used to hang out and joke around together. Now if I joke around with any other girl, she gets really mad. She says that I'm trying to flirt with the other girls. And if she even sees me talking to a girl she starts asking me why I need to talk to her and what I said. It's ridiculous. But I'm really not flirting with these other girls—I'm happy being a couple with Madison. Or at least I *was*."

"It sounds like she's being rather possessive," I said. "Does she seem possessive about her girlfriends? Does she care who *they're* spending time with?"

Justin thought for a moment. "No, I think that she only acts this way with me."

"Well, since you really enjoyed her before the two of you began dating, it might be worth trying to work on the relationship before you end it. What do you think?" I asked.

"Well, I've tried telling her that every time she grills me about talking to another girl, it makes me want to avoid her. That didn't go over too well. Lately I feel like we argue more than we enjoy each other."

I got quiet for a moment. "Honey, my intuition tells me that something else is going on here. That this is not about you, but about what she's witnessed growing up. I feel like she has watched her parents fighting a lot, and so this argumentative style of relationship feels pretty normal to her. Do you know if that's true?"

"Well, I know that her parents are divorced, but that doesn't automatically mean that they always fought a lot. You and Dad didn't argue much at all and you got divorced. In fact I only remember you guys arguing about the divorce, but not much else."

I smiled. "Well I'm glad that your memories of growing up with us are not filled with memories of us fighting. But I think that it's worth asking

Madison for more information about her childhood, before her parents got divorced."

"Why?" Justin asked impatiently. "What does that matter? She's still driving me crazy, and frankly, I don't care if that's because she thinks that arguing a lot is normal. It's not *my* normal."

"Because," I answered, "I think that what happened between her parents is driving a lot of her behavior now. I don't want to say too much because I think if I just hand you all the answers it's not as valuable as you talking to her. Trust me—I think it will be informative."

Justin left my room and reluctantly called Madison. He was on the phone for a long time, and when he found me doing laundry later, he was ready to resume our conversation.

"Okay, Mom. Now I think I know what's going on. Her parents got divorced because her dad kept cheating on her mom. She heard them fighting about it all the time. We talked and figured out that she's probably jealous and possessive because she's worried that I'm going to be like her dad."

"Good job!" I enthused. "I thought that there was more to the story than just her being used to a lot of fighting between couples. So by watching her parents, she learned that men cannot be trusted."

"*All* men?" Justin asked, looking exasperated. "We're not all like her dad!"

"I know that, honey" I soothed. "But she loves her father right? Does she still have a relationship with him?"

"I think it's a strained one, but yes. She lives with her mom but she still talks to her dad and sees him sometimes."

"Well, imagine loving both of your parents but then realizing that one of them has done hurtful things to the other parent, things that broke up the family. Madison has to reconcile the fact that someone she loves has hurt her and her mother. So until she understands that situation better and does some healing on that subject, she's likely to assume that all men will hurt her the way that her dad hurt her and her mother. She's just waiting for it to happen. Because right now, no boy that she meets is going to quickly love her even more than her father who has loved her for her whole life, right? And if her dad loves her that much and still did something so hurtful, then she does not expect loyalty from any man. Does that make sense?"

"Yes, but it sucks!" Justin groaned.

"Yes, it does," I agreed. "But you may be able to make some progress. If she doesn't want to end the relationship with you, then I recommend that you ask her to end her challenging texts and phone calls. Make a boundary that looks like this: If she wants to ask you about a conversation with another girl, then she can acknowledge that her questions are coming from her insecurities and not from inappropriate behavior on your end. If you're not on the defensive every day, I think that you might be more patient with her and willing to help her feel more secure in your relationship. This asks her to notice how much she's being affected by the worries that she picked up from her mother. I'll give you a chance to practice being compassionate with someone that you care about."

Justin looked doubtful. "I don't know if this will work. Do you really think it will?"

I smiled. "Do I think this relationship will last for years and years? No. Let's remember that very few 10th grade romances last more than a few months. But I think that you can learn from this relationship, and you're doing that right now. You're learning that even though someone gets mad at you, it doesn't automatically mean that you're wrong or that she's wrong.

Sometimes a person's reaction is based on your behavior being inappropriate or disrespectful, but sometimes your behavior is fine, and the reaction is because that person has some healing work to do. So in this case, if you're really not flirting with these other girls—"

"I'm not! They're the same girls that I've been friends with since elementary school."

"Okay, then in this case Madison's reaction is alerting her—and you—to the fact that she has some healing work to do. She may or may not do her work—that part we don't know yet. But if you try to help her—to be there for her as she tries to heal this issue—then you will both be better people for having been in this relationship. You know what I mean?"

"Yeah, I do. But relationships seem like a lot of work!" Justin grumbled.

"You know it!" I laughed. "But they offer you some of the largest amounts of positive energy that you'll ever feel. That's why we all crave them even though they're a lot of work and don't always last as long as we would like."

Justin trudged off to have another conversation with Madison. The next few days seemed to go smoothly, with Justin reporting that Madison was less reactive and accusatory with him. But their peace was short-lived, and by the following week, she was once again demanding that Justin stop talking to any girls unless she was there with him. Justin's mood immediately reflected the discord in his relationship, and this time he recognized the mood change and brought it up at the dinner table.

"Mom, Madison is back to asking me about every conversation that I have with a girl, even if it's with her best friend! Who is ugly, by the way."

"Justin!" I chastised. "That's unkind."

"Okay, but I'm just saying—there's no way that I'm trying to pick up her best friend—and yet she's still jealous and bitchy towards me."

"Does she acknowledge that your behavior is okay and that this is about her insecurities?" I asked.

Justin scoffed. "Yeah, sort of, but she says that if I cared about her then I would stop doing things that make her feel insecure. But that seems messed up! That she shouldn't have to change, but I do!"

I knew a teaching moment when I saw it, and I jumped in. "Justin, it sounds like she wants to make you responsible for how she feels. I don't recommend that either of you boys take on that job—for anyone."

Joey put down his fork and joined the conversation. "Wait, what do you mean?"

"Both of you boys are very sweet and compassionate young men. So when someone you care about is upset, you naturally want to help them feel better. But many people think that being in a relationship means that you are then responsible for making the other person happy all the time. This lets the young woman avoid doing her healing work because you learn to tip-toe around sensitive subjects so that your girlfriend stays in a good mood. But this is unhealthy and doesn't make for a balanced relationship."

Justin grinned mischievously. "Are you saying that I should tell her to 'just deal with it' whenever she gets upset?"

I chuckled at him. "You know I'm not saying that, smart ass. What I'm saying is that once you and your girlfriend discover a button that she has—an issue that is painful and needs some healing—then it's up to both of you to work on it, not just you. If she makes her issues your problem, and only your problem, then you're going to resent her."

"Yup, that's where I am!" Justin nodded.

"Then it sounds like it's time to let Madison know that either you work on this issue together, or you go back to being friends. When you two were just friends, it was easier wasn't it?"

"Oh yeah, much easier!"Justin agreed.

I smiled at him. "I think that has to do with the expectations that we each have regarding friendships and romantic relationships. Most people have very different expectations about what each of those should look like. And Madison's expectations of romantic love, at least right now, are not very appealing."

Justin thought for a moment. "Well, I'm ready to admit to the insecurities that *I* have. But I'm not willing to carry hers around anymore. Especially since she acts like I'm a cheater already. I don't like how she makes me feel about myself."

"Well, that's something to notice." I said pointedly. "If someone makes you feel a particular way about yourself, don't dismiss it automatically because it feels uncomfortable. Look at it and feel if there's any truth to it. If there is, own it and address what needs to be changed. Relationships are the perfect place to get clarity about where you stop and the other person begins. Getting and keeping clarity about that is how you develop healthy boundaries."

"Yeah, that makes sense," Justin said thoughtfully, and Joey was nodding his head.

As we cleared the table and did the dishes (okay, I did the dishes, and they just stood there and watched me), we talked about having good boundaries in every relationship.

Justin ended his relationship with Madison a few days after our dinner-time conversation. She was furious with him for a few weeks and encouraged her girlfriends to avoid talking to him as a way of demonstrating their loyalty to her. Justin stayed pretty good-natured about it and even told Madison's friends that he understood if they didn't want to talk to him for awhile. Because he seemed so calm and reasonable, the girls eventually resumed their interactions with Justin, and eventually Madison joined in, not wanting to be left out. Interestingly, today Justin and Madison are very close friends, and they offer each other advice regarding the current romantic relationships that each of them are in.

Chapter 29

Louis' Case – London Calling

My client Louis was calling in from London, England. Many of my clients don't live locally, but I can speak to a client's spirit and read his energy just as well over the phone as I can in person. Louis had originally contacted me regarding a stomach issue he was having that had stumped his doctors. One of his doctors became frustrated with the lack of improvement and declared that Louis' issues were "emotionally based" and dismissed himself from the case. This prompted Louis to ask friends for suggestions about seeing a therapist to heal his emotional issues, and one of them suggested that he talk to me as well.

Louis' spirit had helped him to see that his stomach problems occurred when he worried too much about how his employees perceived him and not enough about how they were performing their jobs. After several sessions about setting and enforcing boundaries, Louis' stomach problems had nearly vanished, and the slight symptoms that occasionally returned let him know when he was sliding back into old habits. Along the way, Louis was thrilled to realize how much guidance his spirit was able to give him regarding each of his employees, and ever since, he'd been calling for what he referred to as "intuitive business consulting."

At the beginning of the phone session, Louis told me about his frustration with his newest hire, a woman who seemed well qualified for the job and made a great impression during her interview.

"This one looked like a sure thing, Christine, so I didn't even run it by you during our last session. She seemed bright, professional, and had a great resume."

"So what's gone wrong?" I asked.

"She has these ideas about what her job should and shouldn't be, and she won't lift a finger to do something outside of what she deems to be her job. Now I'm not talking about asking her to go pick up my dry cleaning or wash my car. I'm talking about asking her to help answer the phones when our receptionist is out sick for the day. The rest of us pitch in, but Molly refuses. So here I am, the boss of the company, answering the phones because one of my employees thinks that it's beneath her job level. And I don't even mind answering the phone, but that sort of attitude and behavior is causing real friction with the other employees, and I can't afford that.

"I've learned since I started working with you that when I'm feeling emotional stress, it's important to regain my balance and sanity, or I'll start getting symptomatic. So I'm asking for guidance from my spirit. I know that I have to fire Molly—that seems obvious at this point—But I want to know how this happened when I thought that hiring this woman was a no-brainer."

While Louis' situation did seem puzzling, I've learned through years of channeling people's spirits that there is always a good reason for each event or circumstance. I'm not always allowed to know what the reason is, but usually my questions are answered, and I'm again reminded of the perfection of the Universe. When I asked Louis' spirit what we could know about this situation, He had a question for Louis.

I asked, "Louis, your spirit wants to know if you remember the difficulty that you had in placing the ad for Molly's position?"

Louis thought for a moment and then chuckled. "Yes! It was the craziest thing. I placed the ad on Craig's List and the phone number was left off. Then I reentered the company phone number, and the rest of the ad disappeared. It took me two days to get that ad to run correctly. Why?"

"Because your spirit is telling me that when something relatively simple encounters multiple stumbling blocks, be open to the idea that the Universe is trying to send you a message."

"What kind of message? Beware of Molly?" he laughed, but I could feel his confusion.

Louis' spirit continued: *"When you are—in your words—going against the flow of the Universe, the Universe will frequently try to assist you by sending you a message. This may come in many forms, such as a diversion, a difficulty in doing what you're attempting to do or a messenger who will mention another option to you. Your job is to pay attention when things do not flow easily, and then be still. Sit quietly and try to feel where things feel too difficult, like you're pushing a boulder up a hill."*

"That sounds a bit impossible to do in the middle of the work day," Louis sounded exasperated. "I can't just close my office door and sit quietly for an hour."

"Only because you're not used to approaching your work in this manner. If someone asked you for a price quote, you'd be willing to tell the customer that you would call him back after you had time to go through the numbers and get a feel for what the job should cost, right?"

"Well, sure," Louis agreed. "But that's different than trying to meditate during the middle of the day in my office."

"I believe that you're using the word 'meditation' because you think that I'm suggesting that you sit quietly for thirty or forty minutes, focusing on emptying your mind. Instead I'm asking you to sit for five or six minutes with the intent to feel where you are and where you are being guided to move."

"That doesn't seem much clearer," grumbled Louis.

"I will keep explaining, but notice how your resistance to what I'm saying is making it harder for you to understand. It literally slows down your mental processing. Picture your energy shoving the new ideas away and only allowing a little bit of information into your mind at a time."

Louis laughed. "He's right! I asked for help, and now I'm shoving it away because I'm afraid that I won't like it. Okay, let's try again."

"What makes it difficult to feel when you're not moving in harmony with the Universe is that the ego gets very attached to the plan that it has and doesn't want to deviate off course. Once you begin moving in a particular direction, say to hire an assistant, then it can be tricky for you to notice the subtle feelings that I'm sending you to let you know that your actions aren't in line with your highest good."

"But how is hiring an assistant not in my highest good?!" Louis demanded defensively. "I was swamped with work, and I know that I needed the extra help."

"Yes, it's true that you needed extra help. But hiring an assistant satisfied your immediate needs, and the Universe was thinking farther ahead. What was being sent to you—and you blocked this person's entry into your life with your ad for an assistant— was a sales director. The next stage of growth for your company involves acquiring larger customers such as Target and Costco, agreed?"

"Yes! Actually, I've had that thought several times lately."

"Yes, I have been sending you that idea/feeling for some time. But your current financial situation is such that you cannot afford to hire both a sales director and an assistant. Once your new sales director lands some large new accounts, then your budget will easily support hiring an executive assistant for yourself and another assistant for the front office."

"Wow." Louis was quiet for a moment. "I'm... humbled by the help that my spirit—and the Universe—was trying to give me," said Louis.

"The Universe is always conspiring on your behalf. When it appears otherwise, it's always because you're not seeing a large enough picture."

Louis' spirit offered him some wording to use in his ad for a sales director so that he could attract the best candidate for the position.

"As usual, I come away from our sessions with a feeling of awe at the Universe's perfection and amazement at my ignorant stumbling and bumbling along!" he chuckled.

The remainder of Louis' session focused on a small area of tension between him and his wife, with his spirit offering suggestions on how Louis could bridge the communication gap they were currently experiencing. At the end of the session, I sent energy to Louis, working long distance to boost his immune system and balance his stomach acids.

Follow-up:

Louis continues to have phone sessions to obtain more "intuitive business consulting." His spirit helped him compose an ad for a sales director, and one was quickly hired and trained. Louis is thrilled with the results of his new sales director, who has generated enough additional revenue to hire two new assistants.

Louis's stomach is no longer used as a messaging system by his spirit, probably because he's become so aware of his emotions that he quickly feels and resolves issues that arise with his employees. Louis' increased awareness has benefitted his marriage as well; his wife says that she now feels that Louis truly hears and understands her.

Chapter 30

Final Chapter – Relationships, Love, & Gratitude

Writing this book in a non-traditional format now presents me with a dilemma. I realize that I'm not sure how to write the final chapter. Because I chose to share some of my clients' stories and my own reflections, there's no "big finish" or resolution to a troubling crisis. So in keeping with the theme of sharing my own understandings, this chapter will be an offering of some of the topics that I'm currently discussing in my daily conversations with my spirit: relationships, love, and gratitude.

Relationships:

People are here to experience themselves through their relationships. We can believe that we are kind, generous, and loving, but only through our relationships can we actually *experience* ourselves as such. Every emotional issue that arises within us begins as a feeling, a negative nudge that something is "off," usually within one of our relationships. If we're fortunate—and brave—we are comfortable addressing that feeling right away and resolving it through conversation and action (if needed). But frequently we ignore the feeling, stuffing it down inside of us because of some rationalization such as: "The time isn't right to bring it up," or "He/She will just get angry," or "There's no point because nothing will change," etc., and so these negative feelings of anger, guilt, worry, sadness, or fear get internalized.

The human body is very accommodating, but it will only store negative energy for so long, and then it begins to send out "notices." Think of these as the warning letter you get reminding you that unless you pay your electric bill soon, you will have your power cut off. These notices are also called symptoms, and we all have them. We get symptomatic when our body is being used by our spirit to tell us that some areas are out of balance in our life and need to be addressed. So when symptoms arise, where should you start focusing your attention? Your relationships.

Clients who have come to see me feeling certain that their stress wasn't related to anyone in their life but was the stress of a demanding schedule, a poor economy, etc, have been surprised to learn that most of their stress is stemming from relationships that need healing/adjusting. Not that outside circumstances aren't stressful—the economy has certainly caused stress for most of us, and an uncertain/unstable work environment can take its toll on the strongest among us. But the stress that seems to result in persistent, stubborn symptoms is typically borne from our relationships that need adjusting.

One relationship that is often overlooked is the relationship that we each have with ourselves. If asked, most people will admit to a fair amount of negative self-talk, of beating up on one's self. The belief, deep down, is that such policing of one's self will keep us from repeating old mistakes. In reality, this self-torture causes everything from ulcers to autoimmune issues. If mentally we attack ourselves constantly, then why shouldn't the body do the same thing? It's an excellent mirror for the damage that we are doing to our psyche.

My own allergies were the physical manifestation of my constant inner critic, who ran amok when I feared that I couldn't be at the top of my class in a top law school. The loving perfection of the Universe is such that as I healed my allergies, I was simultaneously learning to speak more kindly to myself, to motivate myself with something other than threats and criticisms. As my negative self-talk decreased, so did my allergic symptoms, so my allergies became the barometer of my progress on my journey to heal my relationship with myself. Today I have no allergies and a more compassionate relationship with myself, which makes it easier to be compassionate towards others.

Here is a checklist that I use with my clients. As you go through this list, think of all of the people in your life, not just the people that you see every day.

1. Is there anyone in my life currently

who drains me?
- a. If so, is it necessary to have a relationship with her/him?

- b. If so, how can I adjust the relationship so that it is less draining?

2. Is there anyone with whom I'm not comfortable speaking freely?
- a. Is the restriction (on me speaking freely) coming from me or from the other person? In other words, is this fear based on a likely reaction from the other person or on my fears that my past history with other people will repeat itself with this person?

- b. If I journal and get comfortable speaking to this person, will my truth likely be heard?

- c. If I speak my truth—to myself and to this other person—what is the worst that may happen? (Often we work to avoid the worst-case scenario without realizing that we are paying a high price to avoid a result that wouldn't be that terrible.)

3. Is there anyone in my life that makes me want to "play small" and not be

the fullest version of myself that I can be?

   a. If so, is the cost worth keeping the relationship?

   b. Does it feel like I'm betraying myself/damaging my relationship with myself in order to keep a relationship with this person?

4. Is there anyone in my life that requires me to hand over some of my power in order to be in relationship with him/her?

   a. What would it look like if you were to maintain the relationship while respectfully advocating for yourself?

   b. Do you engage in the same dynamic, taking power from others to compensate for the power that this person takes from you? Or are you allowing yourself to be drained of your power/energy and walking around feeling depleted?

It's surprising how often we can sit quietly and ask our body, "What is the message contained in these symptoms?" and receive an answer. The information is there but requires our willingness to hear it.

Love:

While we're children, our parents and the people around us teach us definitions of love. Not the basic, storybook definition of love, but the subtle rules that are not revealed on TV or in romantic movies. Every family has different ideas of what love is and is not, and these ideas are absorbed by the children whether they like them or not. We carry these specific definitions into our adulthood, and since they're usually held subconsciously, we don't even examine them for accuracy. Here are some of the definitions of love that I've collected from the more than 2,000 clients that I've worked with over the past fifteen years.

"Love means that you never go to bed angry."

This may sound like a good idea at first glance, but I once dated a guy who insisted that we stay up until 4 a.m. arguing so that we didn't break this rule because that would mean that we had stopped loving each other. By 4 a.m., I gotta say that I was not feelin' love for anyone (only my bed)!

*"If you love someone then you
don't say anything hurtful."*

Again, this may sound like a lovely idea, but I've seen it lead to couples who are very shut down, not talking about what is bothering them for fear of offending the other person. Resentment builds, and the result is passive/aggressive behavior as each persona acts out the frustration that is not allowed to be spoken. Sometimes the truth is uncomfortable but needs to be (respectfully) said anyway.

I've found that relationships prosper when we create an environment of respect and openness, where the goal is not to monitor every word that you say, but to check your motivation for saying it. *Words seem to cause the most damage when our goal is to be right, to control, or to punish.* If speaking your truth can pass this litmus test of positive intentions, then how the other person decides to react to it is her business. When we take on the responsibility for keeping the other person happy, even if it means sacrificing our truth, the relationship is destined for problems.

> *"If you love someone, then you will do whatever you can to make him or her happy."*

This idea of self-sacrificing one's happiness or sense of empowerment to demonstrate true love has been glorified in romance novels and movies. But I find that in reality, sacrificing one's own dreams to enable someone you love to pursue his/hers, or denying what you want just to keep the peace, usually leads to feeling like a victim or a martyr.

> *"If you love me, then you'll listen to everything that I have to say."*

If you grew up feeling that you were never heard, then you may hold this belief. Your feelings of hurt and smallness were soothed by the belief that someday you would fall in love with someone who would listen to everything that was important to you. This simplistic idea may soothe a small child who feels invisible, but as an adult it can create problems. If you are allowed to rant on for long periods of time and interrupting means that the other person doesn't care about you, then a dynamic is created that is the same as the one you grew up with. Only now you are the one who is blocking the voice of another.

Spirits of various clients have shown me that the healthiest relationships occur when each person is required to practice some emotional containment, refraining from speaking until there is some clarity about what is really at issue. Once you have clarity about what is bothering you, then if your partner interrupts you—to ask a question or to speak his own truth—then you can return to your train of thought without feeling injured by the interruption.

There are thousands of possible rules and definitions regarding love, respect, being a hard worker, a good parent, friend, etc. When your relationships feel extremely heavy, sit quietly and consider which definitions and rules may be limiting your relationships from feeling freer and easier.

Gratitude:

Over the past few months, I've come to revere the concept of gratitude. Little did I know the power this one feeling can have in my life! It has the ability to change my health, my thoughts, and how I feel. If there was a supplement that promised all these benefits, we'd all be taking it!

I confess that when I first started hearing about

gratitude, I brushed it off. I saw it as a lightweight concept, something that made you smile but wasn't powerful enough to transform people's lives and help physical symptoms heal. I was wrong.

My spirit, clever teacher that She is, did not try to lecture me on the importance of gratitude. Instead She made a suggestion: "If you would like to enjoy your life more, please begin noticing how often you are content versus discontented throughout each day." I said, "Sure," assuming that I would experience contentment for the majority of each day. I was mortified to realize that I felt discontent frequently! My spirit whispered the word "discontented" every time I felt frustrated, confused, stressed about time pressures, irritated that I walked upstairs and forgot what I went up there to get, etc, etc. It seemed to be hard to string together twenty minutes in which I felt completely contented!

As if I had been given an addictive puzzle to solve, I began focusing on this idea of contentment throughout each day. I learned that it took a lot to make me happy! I had to have all my relationships going the way that I felt they should be going and all the events in my life unfolding in the way that I deemed best. Well that happened...almost never, so I had a great recipe for feeling discontented.

Now my spirit had my attention. In meditation, I asked Her how I could change things so that I felt contented more often, and Her answer was simple, "Learn to feel gratitude." When I felt confused by this answer She explained,

"Feeling gratitude is easy when things are exactly as you would like them to be. It is more masterful

to be able to feel gratitude whenever you choose. Having the ability to summon gratitude is the same as having the ability to feel happy whenever you wish to do so."

"Okay, I'm in!" I said. "I want to learn how to feel happy in any moment. How do I do this?"

"*Recognize that there will always be elements of your life that are wonderful and elements that are not to your liking. By choosing which elements you focus upon, you choose which emotion to feel.*"

I was already thinking of questions and objections. "But if I just focus on what is going well in my life, then how will I take care of the things that need my attention? I think that if I'm some Pollyanna who says that everything is great when it's not, then I won't change the things that need to get done."

"*There is a big difference between deciding to feel happy by living in denial of what needs to get done and deciding to be happy by addressing the items that are appropriate for you to change and accepting the rest. Did you know that the same skills that made you a good lawyer also made you an unhappy person?*"

"Oh, that's good news!" I laughed. "I'm sure that You're right, since I'm a much calmer, happier person now than I was then. But please—explain.

"*As a lawyer, part of your job was to anticipate any problem that could occur for your clients and write provisions into the contract to protect their interests. This meant that your focus was always on what was wrong or what could go wrong. Now imagine if your job had been very different. Imagine if your job had been to notice and bless every part of*"

*a deal or situation that was not a problem. Do you
see how your focal point would have shifted, and
your energy would have shifted too?"*

"Yes! That sounds like a great job. Because if you
mess up, no one gets in trouble."

*"I have good news for you. If you stay focused on
what is working well in your life, then you will stay
more open and connected to Me, and I will alert you
to things that you should focus on changing. This
doesn't mean that you should live in denial. But you
can notice that something is displeasing and then
choose to appreciate some other facet of your life.
This will help keep you from feeling like a victim of
your life's circumstances. And that is important to
help you feel empowered in your life, which also
leads to feelings of happiness."*

I'm pleased to say that I've taken my spirit's
advice and She was right! Noticing what is right in
a situation does not come as naturally or as quickly
to me as critiquing what is wrong, but I'm making
progress. When I notice that I'm thinking or saying
something negative, I force myself to stop and find
something positive to feel gratitude about. And I
don't let myself fake it, mumbling something like,
"I'm grateful for my health," and continuing forward
with some resentment. I wait until I've landed on a
thought that shifts my mood from grumpy to grateful.

I'm noticing that I'm much happier—the periods
of unhappiness are shorter in duration and occur
less frequently. My relationships are better,
including my relationship with myself. I hated how
negative I used to be sometimes with my boys, like
quickly noticing that they'd done their homework

but focusing instead on the fact that they had left their backpacks in the living room. So first I would critique them, and then I would beat myself up for being a cranky mother. Now I notice what I don't like, but before I complain, I take a breath and notice something else—something positive. This immediately helps me get a better perspective on the irritating stuff and helps me phrase my comments and requests in a softer tone.

So my biggest lesson this year has been this: With some practice, it becomes just as easy to feel gratitude as it does to feel frustration, and so I'm picking the one that feels good! It also carries the additional benefit of making relationships feel easier.

There are many wonderful parts of my life, but the feature that I'm feeling the most grateful for as I write this is the connection that I have with my spirit. My relationship with Her has been life-changing. Through my spirit, I've learned that the Universe is always conspiring to help us, and that when I feel alone and frightened, it is only because I cannot see the whole picture. Thank you, Spirit, for choosing to have this amazing relationship with me/my ego. Thank you for being patient through all my doubts, my accusations that you didn't care, and my worries that you were a figment of my imagination. Thank you for the healing work that I've been honored to help others achieve and for the physical and emotional healing that I've experienced over the past twenty years. And lastly, thank you for being there as I write this book. May it help others to connect more fully to their own spirits.

Appendix – Cause & Effect

————⇒○⟨∅⟩○⇐————

M y clients often ask me where they can find a quick reference guide to help them identify emotional issues that may be contributing to their symptoms. This is my attempt to offer such a tool. There are other teachers who offer detailed explanations of the possible issues that may be reflected within each symptom. This appendix is meant to serve as a starting point, helping the reader begin her exploration of possible mental and emotional factors underlying her symptoms.

I've listed physical symptoms and areas of the body that frequently contain messages. Next to the symptom or body part I've posed some questions to help you begin to uncover the emotional stress or imbalance that may be contributing to your symptom. Sometimes a symptom has a cause that is straightforward and purely physical: If you get food poisoning, it's probably not related to any imbalance in your life—just in your food! But if your symptom is persistent, or doesn't have an obvious physical cause, try reflecting on these questions to see if perhaps your spirit is trying to alert you to some internalized stress that can be resolved.

Allergies:

What harsh statements do I tell myself? (Hint: The statements are usually about yourself. Frequently people are allergic to a set of toxic beliefs or a stream of negative self-talk.)

Adrenal Issues:

What are you racing towards? Will you know when you get there or has racing become a habit? (In cases of adrenal fatigue: Sometimes when people realize that there is no achievable finish line, the adrenal glands stop responding to the habitual sense of urgency.)

Anemia:

What are you not strong enough or good enough to accomplish? Is this really true? Are your goals realistic? Are these your personal goals or the goals that others have set for you?

Arthritis:

Negative emotions cause negative energy throughout the body, and the joints are a place where negative energy seems to collect. Ask yourself: How many of my thoughts each hour are negative, and how many are positive? How can I focus on feeling more gratitude and less frustration?

Back Issues:
    Lower back—How do I feel disempowered? Which issues make me feel ineffective? Which people in my life seem to drain power from me?
    Middle-back—How can I feel more comfortable with myself? How am I unrealistically hard on myself? What would it look like if I was kind and gentle with myself?
    Upper-back—Who can I ask for help when I want to feel more supported? Are there people who want to support me, but they are unsure how? Can I provide some suggestions/coach people so that I can receive better support?

Bladder Problems:
    What fears and issues am I afraid to let go of? Is there an area of my life where I constantly feel like I'm losing control? If I allowed myself to cry over this issue, does it feel like I will never be able to stop crying? (Tip: Allow yourself to cry as you journal about the issue. You will eventually stop crying, and the tears will allow the truth to flood out and provide you with some clarity about moving forward.)

Blood Pressure:
    High—What fears are always lurking in the background for me? Can I bring them up to the surface and either resolve them or release them?
    Low—Which areas of my life cause me to feel defeated because it feels like there will never be

improvement or resolution?

Bowels:
Constipation—In what ways am I stubborn, insisting that things be done my way? How am I holding on to more power than I should be because I'm afraid to let things flow?
Diarrhea—Am I afraid of my lack of power? Are there situations in which I seem to have insufficient control/power?

Ears:
What am I afraid of hearing? (It may be a current fear or a painful criticism from your past that has been triggered)

Eye Problems:
What am I afraid of seeing? What am I trying hard to block/avoid seeing?

Fatigue:
What have I been resisting for a long time? In what areas of my life do I feel a sense of hopelessness?

Gallbladder:
Who do I resent? Which areas of my life cause me to feel resentment? What can I do to feel less resentment?

Inflammation:
What am I inflamed about? What events am I holding onto, replaying them in my mind and keeping myself inflamed?

Liver:

What anger am I storing? What do I accomplish by carrying this deep anger inside of me? How will I know when it's time to let go of the anger (what needs to happen first?)

Shoulders:

How many responsibilities do I really have to carry by myself? Should it all be on my shoulders? Where can I ask for help and delegate? What issues can I turn over to the Universe because there's not much that I can do right now?

Stomach problems:

What part of my life is difficult to digest? What aspects of myself am I having trouble accepting? What would it take for me to become more compassionate towards myself, having more realistic standards and a greater understanding when I make mistakes?

Teeth:

What words do I bite back, refraining from expressing my truth? What would happen if I shared my feelings with the people I care about?

Throat:

What will the repercussions be if I express my true opinions? Who will reject me? Will I be punished? What do I sacrifice by remaining silent in order to "keep the peace" and avoid conflict?

Acknowledgements

―――――⟶∘⟨⟰⟩∘⟵―――――

F requently over the years the spirit world has offered me an image of a spider's web to serve as a metaphor for how we're all interconnected and supported by many unnoticed connections. The web that supported me while I wrote this book is vast, but I wish to give thanks to the people closest to the center.

I want to begin by thanking my parents, whose collective wisdom I draw from continually. They are a beautiful example of commitment, love, and unwavering support. I also want to thank my boys, Joey and Justin, who graciously allowed me to include them in this book, and who never complained about the many hours I spent in front of my computer. Boys, I cherish you. Thank you for choosing me to be your mother; I'm honored and grateful. And to my friends and family members who listened to my ideas, read my personal chapters, and soothed me during my unsure moments, my heartfelt thanks and love. Specifically I wish to thank Sandy, Joe, Thomas, Jill and Dana—my North Carolina support team; you are family in my heart.

The Universe loves to demonstrate It's ability to deliver, and one example occurred the day after I finished writing the first draft of this book. That night I ended my prayers with the request, "Please show me what to do next." The next morning my first client of the day was Carla BeDell, who was in the final stages of publishing her first book. She graciously detailed my first steps and even shared Renee Petrillo, her talented editor. And within the week I met Tammy Bleck while out walking my dog. Tammy is a writer (aka "Witty Woman Writing"), and she took me under her wing and provided both wisdom and wit on many occasions. Thank you Carla and Tammy—your support has been invaluable.

And to my editor Renee: Thank you, thank you, for embarking on this journey with me. I'm amazed at your ability to thoroughly edit my work and yet never have it sound like anything other than my voice. I love that you were frustrated on behalf of my clients when you thought that their spirits were not clear enough, and that you challenged me to further explain myself and the Universe when you weren't satisfied with my written answers. To say that this book is better because of your involvement is an understatement!

I owe deep gratitude to the clients who have trusted me, inviting me into their lives to share a portion of their journey. Because of you I'm able to experience my abilities, and together, we have recognized so many truths. You and your spirits have been delightful teachers, and I am eternally grateful. And to all the masterful teachers that I have studied with, listened to, and prayed with (both alive and in spirit form), I bow in gratitude.

Contacting Christine

To learn more about Christine Lang's work with individual clients, visit her website at www.ChristineLang.org.

If you would like to experience guided meditations created by Christine, visit: www.StressLessMeditations.com

StressLessMeditations.com
online guided meditation

If you're interested in having Christine speak at your workplace or provide intuitive business consulting, visit www.PrismConsulting.org.

PRISM
CONSULTING
See it from
a different angle.

You may also enjoy Christine's blog:
www.ChristineLang,BodyWhispererBlog.com

Made in the USA
Coppell, TX
18 May 2024

32502586R00163